The Story of the 1881 Cumberland Valley Cook and General Recipe Book

1881

With introduction by Tom Kelchner

Jacket copy and introduction (pages 1 - 16) copyright ©2024 by Thomas Kelchner. The *Cumberland Valley Cook and General Recipe Book* is in the public domain.

ISBN: 978-1-7345955-3-6

COOKING / Regional & Ethnic / American / Middle Atlantic States
HISTORY / United States / 19th Century
HISTORY / United States / State & Local / Middle Atlantic (DC, DE, MD, NJ, NY, PA)

Tom Kelchner also is the author of:

To Great Grandmother's House We Go; American Comfort Food from the 1970s, 60s and before

Chicamacomico Cookery, Facsimile Edition

Chicamacomico Cookery, Volume Two, Facsimile Edition

Acknowledgements

I would like to thank several people for their help in the research for this book. Blair L. Williams at the Cumberland County Historical Society was especially helpful digging out the photo of J.B. Morrow and drawing my attention to the 1870s migration of Pennsylvanians to Kansas. Mary Schoedel, the librarian of the John Graham Library in Newville, helped me find many details of the Graham family history. Richard L. Butts of the Newville Historical Society provided me with access to the society's file of information on John Graham.

The Cumberland Valley Cook and General Recipe Book

1881

Introduction

Why did the Kansas Publishing House of Topeka, in 1881, publish a book of recipes from the women of the tiny Cumberland Valley, PENNSYLVANIA, town of Newville? And who was J.A. Graham listed on the cover as "general agent?"

It wasn't like there was any lack of printing presses in Pennsylvania. And shipping books from Kansas 1,000 miles east to their logical market, even by the new railroads of the day, would certainly have eaten into the profit.

It turned out to be a story of nostalgia.

The buyers Graham clearly had in mind were the dozens, perhaps hundreds of families from Cumberland County and other parts of Pennsylvania who emigrated to the new state of Kansas in the 1870s to take advantage of good-quality, cheap land.

It's also a story of the less-than-stellar businessman, Jacob A. Graham (he went by Capt. J.A. Graham) of Newville, Pa., who is listed as "general agent" on the Kansas edition. His printing was basically a reprinting of the second edition of a cookbook published in Pennsylvania by the editor of the *Newville Star and Enterprise* – Graham's brother-in-law. But we are getting ahead of our story

. . .

It all began as an idea for a community cookbook six years earlier.

J.B. Morrow, editor

Photo courtesy of Cumberland County Historical Society

Newspapers have always had the unique ability to gather information by soliciting readers' responses. In June of 1875, J.B. Morrow (1838-1900), editor and publisher of the *Newville Star and Enterprise*, asked his readers to send him their recipes.

Newville wasn't a big place. The 1870 census counted only 907 people living in the borough. There were only scattered farms and tiny villages for 11 miles in any direction. The cookbook project would take advantage of Morrow's printing facility, possibly make some money and build enthusiasm (and readership) for his paper. He announced:

"To the ladies of Newville and Vicinity. In a short time we will have in course of publication a *Home Cook and Recipe Book*. In order that the book shall be of practical value it will contain no recipe but what has been tested, and in order to gain this end we invite contributions from every lady whose eye may happen to catch this notice. Our proposition is that every lady who sends us three or more recipes, written in a plain, legible hand, will receive a copy of the book as soon as published.

"These recipes are not to be confined to cooking merely, but may be of a household nature as well. All ladies are invited to contribute to this book, but this place must have the credit of its getting up, therefore we propose to call it the *Newville Cook and General Recipe Book*.[1]

Morrow, who had been listed as publisher of the *Newville Star and Enterprise*, had taken over the editorship in January of 1870. The paper appeared to be doing well, but, but the previous editor, W.R. Linn, left for a position that offered more "renumeration" and, obviously, Morrow took on the job himself rather than hire another editor.[2] Morrow had edited newspapers in Wyoming earlier in his life. Later, in 1885, he left Newville to take a job as editor of the *Howard County Progress* in Maryland.[3]

Charity and community cookbooks had become a "thing" in Morrow's day. The first one in the United States, *A Poetical Cookbook*, had been published in 1864 in Philadelphia with great success. It was an effort by the women of a sanitary committee to raise money for Union soldiers fighting in the Civil War. The year after Morrow began his project, the first American charity cookbook with a national scope was published. *The National Cookery Book* was a project of the Women's Centennial Committees to raise funds for the 1876 Centennial celebration in Philadelphia. It was a success and went through several reprintings.

By the end of the Nineteenth Century, more than five thousand charity and community cookbooks (CCBs), nearly always published by women's groups, had raised funds for churches, fire companies and political organizations across the nation. Throughout the Twentieth Century, hundreds of thousands were published. They are considered a vast untapped resource for the study of women's history since women across the nation learned organizing and fundraising skills through their cookbook projects. Those skills (and the sales of fundraising cookbooks) would be used to support the temperance and women's suffrage movements.[4]

Morrow's project met with great enthusiasm. In October, 1875, he wrote: "Out of a mass of seven hundred recipes, many of which are duplicated, and some written in an almost illegible hand, and on both sides of the paper, there is necessarily much labor required to get them in shape for the compositor."[5]

In December of 1875 the project was delayed. He wrote: "Owing to our press being occupied with other work we have been unable to keep good our word respecting the Recipe Book. We have it so far advanced however that will enable us to make an early announcement of its completion."[6]

One wonders if Morrow might have finally done the math on his project and realized that completing it meant that he was obligated to give 178 contributors free copies. Those families were probably the chief body of customers for the work. Also, providing 178 copies at 35 cents each (about $10 in today's money) meant he would be giving up more than $1,700 (today's dollars). But he and his staff apparently finished it the next year. By September of 1876 the cookbook was on sale at the News Book Store in Shippensburg, 11 miles west of Newville, for 25 cents (about $7.20 today).[7]

It must have been something of a hit. Three years later, in 1879, newspapers in nearby towns in Cumberland County ran nearly the same item:

"We are in receipt of the second edition of the *Cumberland Valley Cook Book*, published by J. B. Morrow, Newville, Penna. The second edition comes to us with over 200 additional recipes, and we regard It as one of the cheapest cooking compendium extant.

"It is really the combined culinary wisdom of the ladies of the valley, whose names are published in the book in alphabetical order. Price, sent by mail, 35 cts. Address as above."[8]

Today, facsimile editions of an *1881 Cumberland Valley Cook and General Recipe Book by the Ladies of the Cumberland Valley, Pennsylvania* are available on line. Morrow's name is not on that edition. Instead, "J.A. Graham" is listed as the "general agent."

In Morrow's obituary in August of 1900, Mrs. J.A. Graham of Walnut Street, Carlisle, is listed as his sister.[9] Thus, "general agent" J.A. Graham was Morrow's brother-in-law.

Capt. J.A. Graham and the Kansas connection

Jacob Alter Graham (Sept. 30, 1832–June 6, 1910), always referred to as "Capt. J.A. Graham," was a colorful figure in Cumberland County and there were frequent newspaper mentions of him. According to his obituary: "He had been a captain of cavalry during the (Civil) war and was severely wounded in one of the numerous engagements in which he participated."[10]

According to Civil War era records, he joined the 13th Pennsylvania Cavalry, 117 Volunteers[11] as a lieutenant and was discharged as a captain. The unit saw action from 1861 until nearly the end of the war with the Army of the Potomac, mostly in Virginia.

His brother George W. Graham (b. Dec 6, 1840) had enlisted in the same unit. He was killed May 16, 1863. "He fell in a skirmish with the rebels near Ashby Gap, Virginia," according to the record of deaths in a Graham family bible reproduced in a photo copy in the possession of the Newville Historical Society.

In March, 1865, one month before the end of the war, the 13th joined the "Military Division Mississippi" and remained there until July, 1865. It must have been there -- "out west" as one source mentioned -- that Captain Graham was wounded. Since he lived to be 77, he clearly overcome whatever health issues he suffered in the war.

He seemed to have been involved in a lot of ventures that lasted only a short time. An 1893 piece in the *Carlisle Sentinel* about Graham visiting his brother in Newville said he "...will be remembered by our older citizens. He at one time was a prominent democrat in the county, and in the contest for sheriff nomination when Sheriff Fereman was successful, came in second in the race.

"The captain is a jovial, whole-souled gentleman and takes great pride in his native county."[12]

An 1886 "personal" column noted that Graham had red hair earlier in life. It had turned gray at that point (he would have been 53), but he was in good condition and was looking as well as he had forty years in the past.[13]

Captain J.A. Graham left Newville in 1880 and moved to Kansas. Apparently, he had lived there before the Civil War.[14] An 1881 news story in the *Chambersburg Valley Spirit* reported that: "On Monday night, January 2d, the meat market of Captain J. A. Graham, of Winfield, Kansas, was destroyed by fire, with its contents, entailing loss of upwards of $300 (about $9,000 in 2023 dollars). Captain Graham removed from Newville last Fall to the above place, and had fairly gotten under way when this calamity befell him."[15]

Apparently, he overcame that catastrophe, at least for a while. He was still advertising the meat market in August of that year.[16]

The Honorable John Graham and Newville's long-delayed bequest

Photo courtesy of the John Graham Library

The brother that Capt. Graham frequently visited, the Honorable John Graham (Aug. 4, 1843-Dec. 15, 1915), was one of the wealthiest men in the region. The two Graham brothers were descendants of Jared Graham who immigrated from Northern Ireland and purchased land in what would become Cumberland County from the Penn family in 1731.[26] John "... received a commercial education at Eastman's College, Poughkeepsie, N. Y."[27] and served in the Pennsylvania state legislature 1882-86. He made his fortune in various ventures, including a tannery in Newville then trolly companies in Pennsylvania, Illinois and West Virginia.

According to his death story: "In the early nineties and for a period of a dozen years or more he was actively engaged in the trolley business. In 1890 he bought the lines of the Wyoming Traction Company at Wilkesbarre (sic). They were not in good shape and were disconnected. He merged them and made them pay.

Later, he became connected with a street railway system at Bloomington, Illinois.

"In 1902-1903 he was prominently identified with a syndicate that operated the Camden Interstate Railways (electric) at Huntingdon, West Virginia, and was connected in an executive capacity with the American Telephone company, was a director the Consolidated Telephone Company, of Eastern Pennsylvania, a director of the First National Bank of Newville." [28]

In 1908, he was listed as the president on an advertisement for the sale of bonds for the Cumberland Railway Company, a trolly company that provided service from Newville to Mount Holly Springs. [29]

After a long illness he underwent surgery at Johns Hopkins Hospital in Baltimore in December, 1915, but did not survive the procedure. [30]

At the time of his death "his business interests were varied and he is the owner of ten of the largest farms in the state and, had a considerable fortune in stocks, bonds and other property."[31] Graham left a fortune of $300 - $400,000 ($9 to $12 million in 2023 dollars) in a trust that was to provide its income and interest to his third wife Kathrine (Cartmell) Graham (1855-1962) until her death. The will also stipulated bequests to numerous beneficiaries, including sums for a YMCA in Newville, a library (today the John Graham Library), the Big Spring Presbyterian Church (where he and his first two wives are buried in the John Graham Memorial Cemetery) and a hospital (Newville's Graham Medical Clinic).[32] Katherine Graham is buried in Winchester, Va.,

Newville had to wait a long, long time to get the benefits. Katherine lived to be 93 and didn't die until 1962! At that point the trust was worth $265,000 ($2.7 million in 2023 money),[33] still quite enough to endow the institutions he named. The library also received Graham's residence on Parsonage Street.

"It was Mr. Graham's desire to confer a benefit upon the town of Newville and the surrounding country and he believed that a well selected library is a great help and aid in assisting the formation of broad and correct habits of life."[34]

Graham's move to Kansas certainly explains why the *Cumberland Valley Cook and General Recipe Book by the Ladies of the Cumberland Valley, Pennsylvania*, was published in Topeka. Once there, he obviously saw a market.

Graham wasn't the only Pennsylvanian to immigrate to the new state of Kansas in the 1870s. Kansas had become a U.S. territory in 1854 and a state in 1861. In the lead up to the Civil War, the volatile issue of whether Kansas would become a slave or free state led to massive violence there and the nickname "bleeding Kansas."

By the 1870s, memories of the Civil War were still fresh in everyone's mind, but even fresher were the visions of new railroads and cheap land. That attracted lots of Pennsylvanians, including some from Cumberland County.

After he arrived, Graham surely saw transplanted Pennsylvanians as a market for a book of recipes from the "ladies of Cumberland County, Pennsylvania."

The Pennsylvania immigration in Kansas

According to a research paper by Pennsylvania state archivist George R. Beyer,[35] a group of Pennsylvania German people from Cumberland County in 1872 moved to Ellsworth and Russel counties in the center of Kansas. The expedition was organized the previous year by members of the German Baptist Church (today called the Church of the Brethren). In April of 1872 the settlers traveled by rail from Harrisburg. The German Baptist Brethren who settled near Wilson. Kansas, named their area "Pennsylvania."[36] Today it is a town of 13,000.

It appears that at least some kept in touch with friends and family in Newville. In the cookbook, Mrs. M.J. Killian and Mrs. Ida Martin of Wilson are two of the four Kansas residents listed as contributors.

In 1878 the *Harrisburg Daily Patriot* reported that nine rail coaches of emigrants from "points along the Cumberland Valley Railroad," left Harrisburg for Kansas.[37] The Cumberland Valley Railroad ran through Cumberland County from Harrisburg then to Winchester, Va.

Kansas census records showed that by 1880, 59,236 residents of the 996,000 in that state – nearly 17 percent – had been born in Pennsylvania![38]

It isn't known if he got permission to publish Morrow's book or if he just helped himself to it. It's probable that the original had no registered copyright, so, it really didn't matter. There doesn't seem to be any record of a copyright on the U.S. Copyright Office web site. Community and charity cookbooks have usually been very small ventures and not registered.

Graham moved back to Pennsylvania the next year. In June of 1882, a Harrisburg paper reported: "Capt. J.A. Graham, of Newville, has taken charge of the Mullin house at Mt. Holly Springs, and that popular hotel now opened for the reception of summer guests."[17]

An advertisement for the hotel said it: "has changed hands and been put into first-class condition for the season of 1882. Situated at the mouth of a deep gap in the mountain five miles south of Carlisle, the location is excellent, the scenery grand, the house large, well ventilated and specially adapted to the convenience and comfort of guests.

"The Menu excellent, liquors choice. Billiards, bowling alleys, fishing, boating, driving and other means of enjoyment and exercises."[18]

Mount Holly Springs is in a gap in South Mountain where Mountain Creek flows. In summers the area is a pleasant, cool and shady spot.

The Depression of 1882-85

"The Depression of 1882–1885 was not inaugurated by financial disaster or mass panic, but was rather an economic downturn that came about through a protracted and gradual process. The downturn was preceded by a period of prosperity over the years 1879 to 1882, a growth powered by expansion of the American railroad industry and the opening of economic opportunities associated with the development of the transportation system.

"In 1882 this trend reversed, resulting in a decline in railroad construction and a decline in related industries, particularly iron and steel. Mismanagement and rate wars negatively affected profitability and the luster of railroads as an investment was dulled; money dried up and construction of new lines was negatively impacted..."[39]

Graham appears to have been in the hotel business for only one season. There are advertisements for the Holly Hotel as late as October of that year, but none afterward. The following year, he appealed the property assessment, indicating that he had purchased the property.[19] The timing for his hotel venture couldn't have been worse. The depression of 1882-85 had begun in March.[20]

In 1889, Graham was living in Washington, D.C., and was appointed superintendent of the Washington Asylum. The *Carlisle Sentinel* wrote: "Capt. Graham is well fitted for the position, and no doubt will give satisfactory service to the 'powers that be.'"[21]

It appeared that the job only lasted about two years. In 1902, Graham was back in Carlisle and involved in yet another business venture. In April of that year, he and D.L. McDermott demonstrated a level and plumb-board device. The *Sentinel* reporter wrote "the instrument can be used to great advantage by railroad men, cabinet makers, stone masons, brick layers, street commissioners and others; the device was patented by Mr. McDermott and Capt. J.A. Graham on January 29th, 1902. The object of this morning's exhibition was to interest citizens or others in the matter of their manufacture, Carlisle being spoken of as the place for the factory."

Graham died in Washington, D.C., in June of 1910. He was buried in Arlington National Cemetery.[22]

The cookbook

The book we have is an 1881 printing of an original community cookbook from 1876, which was revised in 1878 or 9. Many of the recipes are merely lists of ingredients – which was typical of that day. The list of contributors and failure to list their names with their recipes seems to indicate that Morrow wanted to get names in print to appeal to the readership. Or possibly he did it to save space. It was more marketing than cookbook design.

HOWEVER, as peculiar as the volume is as a cookbook, it is a fantastic catalog of the popular recipes of the day, at least in Newville, Pa. If eight contributors submitted recipes for pound cake (the first entry) and 19 send their recipes for fruit cake (second entry), one can probably conclude that pound cake and fruit cake were popular in that area (and possibly the U.S.) in that day.

D.L. McDermott

> **CARLISLE PAPER STOCK CO**
> No. 225 and 227 East Chapel Avenue.
> D. L. MCDERMOTT, Manager.
> E. M. SPANGENBERG, Sec. & Treas.
> **HIGHEST CASH PRICE** paid for Rags,
> Gum, Iron, Copper, Brass, Zinc, Lead, etc,
> MOTTO:—Honest weight and fair dealing,
> 12a1m

1902 display ad for McDermott's business[40]

David L. McDermott, (1841- Aug. 20, 1912) was the manager of a junk business located in the 200 block of East Chapel Alley in Carlisle.[41] He appears to have been something of an inventor. Before his work on the leveling device, in 1900, he "... made formal application for a patent on his new rifling process for projectiles."

Apparently, he also had a son with a drinking problem. He ran the following notice n 1908:

"Notice to liquor Men and Others. Notice is hereby given to all persons not to sell nor give any Intoxicating liquor to my son, Charles McDermott, under penalty of the law. D. L, McDermott."[42]

He also was involved in third-party politics. He was one of four men in Carlisle who filed the paperwork to run a candidate from the obscure "Lincoln Party" in the election in 1906.[43]

According to his obituary, McDermott died at home of heart disease. The obituary was titled: "War veteran dies of heart disease." The piece also said he had served in Company K, 107 Pennsylvania Volunteers.[44] There is no record of him in the pacivilwar.com list of those who served in that company. Similarly, he is not listed in the National Park Service Solders and Sailors Database. In 1910, an article ran that might indicate he had only claimed to be a veteran:

> "WANTS PENSION RESTORED
> "Congressman Olmsted Acts in Behalf of Carlisle Man
>
> "Washington D. C, April 27. RepresentativeOlmsted, yesterday presented a resolution directing the House committee on invalid pensions to investigate and report why David L. Mc-Dermott, of Pennsylvania, has been deprived since 1902 of his pension of $24 n month, granted him by a special act of Congress, July 6, 1886. This pension was suspended by the commissioner of pensions under charges that fraud have been practiced in securing it."[45]
>
> A monthly pension of $24 in 1902 would be about $860 in 2023 dollars.

The oldest known recipes for shoo fly pie?

On page 45, there are two recipes for shoo fly pie (one is really a cake). They might be the oldest known recipes for the long-popular Pennsylvania dish.

Shoo-fly pie, a molasses and crumb breakfast dish, was an invention of Pennsylvania and has a well-documented 140-year history. What is widely believed to be the quintessential Pennsylvania Dutch pie probably evolved from a "Centennial cake" that was created — possibly by a New York City chef — for the Centennial Celebration in Philadelphia which opened May 10, 1876, according to Pennsylvania food historian William Woys Weaver.[23] If this is so, then the two recipes that Morrow obtained from the housewives in Cumberland County were from the time of the invention of the dish. News articles about the second edition in April, 1879, indicated that 200 recipes had been added to the original. The shoo fly pie recipes were probably among them if Weaver is correct.

The unique nature of the *Cumberland Valley Cookbook* — its "survey" format of multiple examples of popular recipes — hints that shoo-fly pie and cake were new in the day. There was only one recipe for each.

References to "Centennial pie" and shoo-fly pie appeared in newspaper lists of county fair pie-baking contest winners in the 1880s in Columbia and Union counties. Early newspaper references to it are all from Pennsylvania,

Previously, the oldest known recipe for shoo-fly pie was found in a source from Northeastern Pennsylvania dated to about 1890. Boston-based food historian Mark H. Zanger, writing in the *Oxford Encyclopedia of Food and Drink in America*, said "shoo-fly cake" and "shoo-fly pie" recipes appeared in the *Talent Cook Book* published by the Grace Evangelical Lutheran Church in Mount Carmel in Columbia County.

. . .

The Cumberland Valley cookbook itself is basically a list of dishes with numbered lists of recipe variations. For example, the first one, Marble Cakes, lists eight recipes. The second, fruit cakes, lists 19.

Major chapters are:

- Cakes
- Icings
- Puddings
- Creams, Custards, Etc.
- Pies
- Eggs
- Bread
- Meats
- Fish
- Soups
- Sauces
- Ketchups
- Pickles
- Corn, Vegetables, Etc.
- Salads, Etc.
- Canned Fruit
- Preserves, Fruits, Jellies, Etc.
- Miscellaneous

The miscellaneous section contains advice for everything from carpet patching and snakebite treatment to the removal of cancerous warts.

There is an index, organized by type of recipe, on pages 67-69.

The 1881 version, which we assume was Capt. J. A. Graham's project, didn't seem to have been proof read by a writing professional. There are extraneous numbers at the bottom of pages 17, 33 and 49. Those are glaring and easy-to-spot typographic errors which any experienced editor (like Morrow) surely would have caught. That suggests that Graham had a copy of Morrow's original book, handed it to a printer in Kansas with instructions to print it. The printer would have hand set the type since typesetting machinery was not developed until the end of the 1880s.[24] In that world, printers would pull "galley proofs" from the hand-set type and give them to the customer to proof read. It appears that Graham skipped that step or didn't do a very good job of it.

Origins of the recipes

A few of the recipe names seem to suggest their source:

Feather Cakes, pp 15, #2 "Kate's Feather Cake."

Aunt Jemima's Cake, pp 26 (Probably named for a popular minstrel show tune of trhe day. Aunt Jemima pancake mix, America's first ready-mix food, didn't appear until 1889)[25]

Miss Barton's Cake, pp 26 (American Red Cross founder Clara Barton?)

Wm. D. Gobrecht's Favorite Lemon Pie (Jan. 24, 1858), pp 42 (He was a notable Adams County insurance company president).

Patent Gas Sherbet – "the best and healthiest drink in use," pp 61

For all its convoluted history, the *Cumberland Valley Cookbook* is a wonderful little volume. It's a record of everyday kitchen-tested recipes from the 1870s, from the readers of the tiny little *Star and Enterprise* in the tiny little Pennsylvania town of Newville.

There appears to be only one surviving copy, so, "General Agent" J.A. Graham, for all his history, gave us something valuable when he reprinted it in Kansas for ex-Pennsylvanians who might welcome recipes with a taste of home.

Endnotes

1 "Farm and Housewife," *Star and Enterprise*, Newville, Pa., June 1, 1875, pp 5
2 "Newspaper Changes," *Star and Enterprise*, Newville, Pa., Jan. 22, 1870, pp 3
3 Ibid
4 Longone, Janice B., "Cookbooks and Manuscripts," *The Oxford History of Food and Drink in America*, (New York: Oxford University Press, 2004), V. 1, pp 291
5 *Star and Enterprise*, Newville, Pa., Oct. 5, 1875, pp 5
6 "Town and Country," *Star and Enterprise*, Newville, Pa., Dec. 21, 1875, pp 5
7 "Valuable Cookbook," *News-Chronicle*, Shippensburg, Pa., Sept. 9, 1876, pp 3
8 "The Cook Book," *News-Chronicle*, Shippensburg, Pa., Apr. 26, 1879, pp 2
9 "John B. Morrow," *Carlisle Evening Herald*, Carlisle, Pa., Aug. 22, 1900, pp 4
10 "Capt. Graham Dead," *Carlisle Evening Herald*, Carlisle, Pa., June 7, 1910, pp 1
11 https://www.nps.gov/civilwar/search-soldiers-detail.htm?soldierId=158948A2-DC7A-DF11-BF36-B8AC6F5D926A
12 "Personal," *Sentinel*, Carlisle, Pa., June 14, 1893, pp 3
13 "Personal," *Weekly Herald*, Carlisle, Pa. Dec. 21, 1886, pp 1
14 *History of Cumberland and Adams Counties, Pennsylvania*, (Chicago: Warner, Beers and Co, 1886), section 451
15 "In other Counties," *Valley Spirit*, Chambersburg, Pa., Feb. 9, 1881, pp 2
16 "Meat Market," *Courier*, Winfield, Kan., Aug. 4, 1881, pp 1
17 "Carlisle and Cumberland," *Daily Independent*, Harrisburg, Pa., June 5, 1882, pp 1
18 "Mt. Holly Springs Hotel," *Weekly Herald*, Carlisle, Pa., Aug. 24, 1882, pp 4
19 "Appeals," *Chronicle*, Shippensburg, Pa., March 16, 1883, pp 2
20 https://en.wikipedia.org/wiki/Depression_of_1882%E2%80%931885 (accessed Sept. 14, 2023)
21 "Gossip," *Sentinel*, Carlisle, Pa., Dec. 13, 1889, pp 1
22 "Capt. Graham Passes On," *Valley Times-Star*, Newville, Pa., June 09, 1910, pp 5
23 Weaver, William Woys; *Pennsylvania Dutch Country Cooking*," (New York: Abbeville Press, 1993), pp 96
24 https://library.fandm.edu/c.php?g=750623&p=5376003#:~:text=Mechanical%20typesetting%20began%20in%20the,a%20set%20of%20brass%20matrixes. (accessed Oct. 22, 2023)
25 "Aunt Jemima," *The Oxford History of Food and Drink in America*, (New York: Oxford University Press, 2004), V. 1, pp 52
26 Rupp, I.D., *History of Dauphin, Cumberland, Perry, Bedford, Adams and Franklin Counties, Pa.*, (Lancaster, Pa.: Gilbert Hills, Proprietor and Publisher, 1946) pp 451
27 *History of Cumberland and Adams Counties, Pennsylvania*, (Chicago: Warner, Beers & Co., 1886), section 451
28 "John Graham of Newville Dies," *Sentinel*, Carlisle, Pa., Dec. 16, 1915, pp 4
29 "Bonds," *Shippensburg Chronicle*, Shippensburg, Pa., June 17, 1909, pp 3
30 Ibid
31 "Former Assemblyman Dies in Baltimore Following Operation," *Evening Herald*, Carlisle, Pa., Dec. 16, 1915, pp 1
32 "Newville Generously Remembered in Will of Late John Graham," *Carlisle Evening Herald*, Carlisle, Pa., Jan. 14, 1916, pp 1

33 "Mrs. John Graham Dies; Articles of Will Studied," *Valley Times-Star*, Newville, Pa, Sept. 27, 1962, pp 1
34 Ibid
35 Beyer was an Assistant Archivist at the Pennsylvania Historical and Museum Commission's Division of Public Records
36 Beyer, George R., *Pennsylvania Germans Move to Kansas*, masters thesis, Cornell University, 1961, pp 31
37 Ibid, pp 34
38 Ibid, pp 26
39 Ibid
40 "Carlisle Paper Stock Company," *Carlisle Evening Herald*, Carlisle, Pa., Aug. 27, 1902, pp 1
41 Ibid
42 "Notice to Liquor Men and Others," *Sentinel*, Carlisle, Pa., Jan. 23, 1908, pp 3
43 "New Lincoln Party," *Evening Herald*, Carlisle, Pa., Nov. 20, 1905, pp 4
44 "War Veteran Dies of Heart Disease," *Carlisle Evening Herald*, Carlisle, Pa., Aug. 21, 1912, pp 1
45 "Wants Pension Restored," *Carlisle Evening Herald*, Carlisle, Pa., Apr. 29, 1910, pp 1

THE CUMBERLAND VALLEY COOK

AND GENERAL

RECIPE BOOK,

BY THE

LADIES OF THE CUMBERLAND VALLEY, PENNSYLVANIA.

OVER 700 RECIPES.

J. A. GRAHAM, TOPEKA, KANSAS,
GENERAL AGENT.

Copyright applied for.

TOPEKA, KANSAS:
KANSAS PUBLISHING HOUSE.
1881.

THE CUMBERLAND VALLEY

COOK

AND GENERAL

RECIPE BOOK.

BY THE LADIES

OF THE

CUMBERLAND VALLEY, PENNSYLVANIA.

OVER 700 RECIPES.

TOPEKA, KANSAS:
KANSAS PUBLISHING HOUSE.
1881.

TO THE PUBLIC.

It is with pleasure that we place this edition of the CUMBERLAND VALLEY COOK AND GENERAL RECIPE BOOK before the people. We have received a cloud of testimonials, all attesting its value as a housekeeper's companion. And why should it not be? The recipes contained herein are results of experience and careful tests. No lady will have a set of recipes unless she knows them to be good, and every lady who has contributed to this book has sent us her best recipes. How often it occurs that we find a lady pretty well advanced in life before she has gathered together enough of favorite recipes to subserve her purpose. After years of examination, study and practical tests, she finds she has about what she wants. How different now! Our book comes in as a labor-saving machine. You have but to turn to its pages and you have the wisdom and experience of not only one lady, but the combined culinary sagacity of hundreds of ladies. Then think, too, of the *love* that has gone into these recipes. Every good wife who stands over steam, and perspires around a cook-stove, is actuated by the highest motives. She is stimulated to do so out of an affectionate regard for her husband, and she taxes her ingenuity to the utmost to bring to the highest perfection that art which is so intimately interwoven with her domestic life. But enough. Let the book stand on its own merits. It must speak for itself. Its own practical usefulness must confirm our words.

OUR CONTRIBUTORS.

Abrahims, Miss Annie.................................Altoona, Pa.
Abrahims, Mrs. Henrietta........................Allen, Pa.
Allen, Mrs. Elizabeth.............................Bloserville, Pa.
Alexander, Miss Agnes E........................ " "
Alexander, Mrs. Maggie .... " "
Allen, Miss Lucy E...................................Newville, Pa.
Askin, Mrs. Carrie.................................... " "
Au, Miss Jennie E....................................Newburg, Pa.
Au, Mrs. John C...Dahlgren, Ill.
Au, Miss Mary C...Newburg, Pa.
Barnes, Miss Olive...................................Washburne, Ill.
Barr, Mrs. Emma...Newburg, Pa.
Barto, Miss Ella R....................................Newville, Pa.
Blean, Miss Emma................................... " "
Bloser, Mrs. M. E....................................Bloserville, Pa.
Boak, Mrs. P. J..Pine Glen, Pa.
Bowers, Mrs. Adam..................................Newville, Pa.
Boyles, Mrs. Atchison .... " "
Boyles, Mrs. L. B................................... " "
Brewster, Miss Nina R........................ " "
Brewster, Miss N. W............................. " "
Brandon, Mrs. Mary E........................... " "
Bricker, Mrs. W. C............................... " "
Brown, Mrs. L. B.....................................Sannemin, Ill.
Burkhart, Mrs. J. S...............................Bloserville, Pa.
Cameron, Miss Minnie.............................Altoona, Pa.
Chorpening, Mrs. A. L..........................Bloserville, Pa.
Cook, Mrs. A. J..Bellefonte, Pa.
Cratzer, Miss Annie...............................Newville, Pa.
Crawford, Miss Annie G....................Huntingdon, Pa.
Crawford, Mrs. A. E............................ " "
Crawford, Mrs. Porter......................... " "
Davidson, Miss Lizzie............................Newville, Pa.
Davidson, Miss Sophia P...............Washington, D. C.
Davidson, Mrs. J. B................................Newville, Pa.
Davidson, Mrs. Jane Ann...................Kerrsville, Pa.
Daelhousen, Mrs. F. E............................Triumph, Pa.
Deihl, Mrs. Laura...................................Maroa, Ill.
Derr, Miss Zillie......................................Newville, Pa.
Diller, Miss Annie L..............................Bloserville, Pa.
Diller, Miss Maggie................................Newville, Pa.
Dock, Mrs. Jacob....................................Martinsburg, Va.
Doirne, Miss Sophia...............................Triumph, Va.
Ege, Mrs. Col...Greensburg, Va.
Elliott, Miss Beckie...............................Carlisle, Pa.
Elliott, Mrs. Emma J.............................Newville, Pa.
Elliott, Mrs. Mary C............................. " "
Ensminger, Miss Amanda C..................Bloserville, Pa.
Ensminger, Mrs. Jennie........................Newville, Pa.
Evans, Mrs. Nettle................................Liberty, Mo.
Ferris, Mrs. E. M....................................Newville, Pa.
Fickes, Miss Lizzie................................ " "
Fickes, Miss Susanna........................... " "
Filey, Miss Laura C...............................Carlisle, Pa.
Firestine, Miss Annie M......................Newville, Pa.
Fosnot, Mrs. Harry................................. " "
Frymire, Miss Annie M......................... " "
Gayman, Miss Annie...............................Bloserville, Pa.
Gobrecht, Mrs. Clara J........................Altoona, Pa.
Gilmore, Miss Lydia..............................Newville, Pa.
Gorley, Miss Bessie............................... " "
Graham, Mrs. J. A....................................Denver, Col.
Green, Miss Bell....................................Carlisle, Pa.
Gutshall, Miss Lizzie............................Newville, Pa.
Haldeman, Mrs. Dr...................................Paola, Kas.
Hall, Miss May C......................................Kerrsville, Pa.
Hannon, Miss Laura..................................Newville, Pa.
Hazzard, Miss Gussie..............................Huntingdon, Pa.
Heberlig, Miss Maggie............................Newville, Pa.
Hefflebower, Miss Addie..................... " "
Hemminger, Miss Mattie E................. " "
Herron, Miss Lilla ....Washington, D. C.
Herron, Miss Maggie B....................... " "
Herron, Mrs. R. S....................................Princeton, Ill.
Hershey, Mrs. Mary................................Altoona, Pa.
High, Mrs. Lizzie....................................Newville, Pa.
Huntsberger, Miss Lizzie................... " "
James, Mrs. E.. " "
Kamarer, Mrs. Wm..................................Bloserville, Pa.
Kelley, Miss Annie.................................McGraw, Pa.
Killian, Mrs. M. J..................................Wilson, Kas.
King, Miss Maggie E............................Newville, Pa.
Koser, Mrs. L. C....................................Doubling Gap, Pa.
Lamberton, Miss Beckie J...................Carlisle, Pa.
Laughlin, Mrs. John..............................Newville, Pa.
Lay, Miss Ellie V................................. " "
Lecky, Miss Sarah..................................Bloserville, Pa.
Leidigh, Miss Annie R.........................Newville, Pa.
Leidigh, Mrs. T. F..................................Hutchinson, Kas.
Lenney, Miss M. J..................................Newville, Pa.
Lewis, Miss Ella.................................... " "
Lewis, —— S. J....................................Dickinson, Pa.
Long, Mrs. A. J.......................................Newville, Pa.
Lindsay, Miss Bessie L........................ " "
Long, Mrs. A. J.................................... " "
Martin, Mrs. Ida.....................................Wilson, Kas.
Martz, Miss Alice..................................Middle Spring, Pa.
Martz, Mrs. J. C....................................Newville, Pa.
Mason, Mrs. Kate....................................North East, Pa.
Maxwell, Mrs. M. J................................Newville, Pa.
Meck, Mrs. Margaret.............................Carlisle, Pa.
McCaleb, Miss Bell S............................Newville, Pa.
McCandlish, Miss Alice....................... " "
McCandlish, Miss M. M........................ " "
McCord, Miss Annie................................North East, Pa.
McCord, Miss Sue...................................Philadelphia, Pa.
McCullough, Miss Jane..........................Big Spring, Pa.
McCullough, Miss Nancy J.................. " "

McCullough, Mrs. A. B...............Stoughstown, Pa.
McCullough, Mrs. E...................... " "
McCullough, Mrs. Samuel..................Newville, Pa.
McElwain, Mrs. J. S...............New Hartford, Iowa.
McElwain, Miss Lizzie.......................Newville, Pa.
McIvor, Mrs. Nettie.......................... " "
McLaughlin, Miss Maggie.................Dickinson, Pa.
Morrow, Mrs. J. B.............................Newville, Pa.
Mowry, Mrs. P. H..............................Chester, Pa.
Moyer, Mrs. Sarah Ellen...................Kerrsville, Pa.
Myers, Miss Catherine......................Orrstown, Pa.
Myers, Mrs. John...........................Bloserville, Pa.
Murphy, Miss Emma........................Newville, Pa.
Ployer, Miss Kate E.......................Bloserville, Pa.
Ployer, Mrs. Kate E.............................Altoona, Pa.
Reifsneider, Mrs. William................Newville, Pa.
Rhinehart, Miss Ella..........................Carlisle, Pa.
Rhoads, Miss Lily..............................Newville, Pa.
Robinson, Mrs. R. E.......................... " "
Rupp, Mrs. Mary A..................Shiremanstown, Pa.
Saltsman, Miss Mattie E..............Harrisburg, Pa.
Sanderson, Miss Ella........................Newville, Pa.
Sanderson, Mrs. Wm......................... " "
Sayer, Miss Kate.......................Washington, D. C.
Scouller, Mrs. Aggie E....................Newville, Pa.
Sharp, Mrs. Martha........................ " "
Sharp, Mrs. Wm.......................Washington, D. C.
Shoemaker, Mrs. H. C.....................Moshannon, Pa.
Shoemaker, Mrs. W. B......................Newville, Pa.
Shillito, Mrs. M..................................Triumph, Pa.
Shrom, Mrs. Geo................................Newport, Pa.
Slaybaugh, Miss Annie......................Newville, Pa.
Smith, Mrs. Agnes D........................ " "
Smith, Mrs. J. W...............................Dickinson, Pa.
Smith, —— Wilhelmina..................Plainfield, Pa.

Souders, Mrs. Maria.......................Bloserville, Pa.
Spangler, Mrs. Theo. M.................White House, Pa.
Stevick, Mrs. D. B............................Newburg, Pa.
Stewart, —— Margaretta..................Newville, Pa.
Stewart, Miss Mary........................Moshannon, Pa.
Storms, Mrs. Sarah............................Triumph, Pa.
Stough, Mrs. Thos............................Newville, Pa.
Stroman, Miss Kate........................... " "
Thomas, Mrs. D. N............................ " "
Thomson, Miss Mary A....................Carlisle, Pa.
Thomson, Mrs. Rose S....................... " "
Tritt, Mrs. Geo. W..............................Newville, Pa.
Turner, Miss Kate..........................Greensburg, Pa.
Tuttle, Miss Annie M......................North East, Pa.
Utley, Mrs. Sallie...............................Newville, Pa.
Vanhorn, Mrs. Mary............................Triumph, Pa.
Vanard, Mrs. Wm..............................Newville, Pa.
Wagner, Miss Alice B...................Hockersville, Pa.
Wagner, Mrs. John C....................Shippensburg, Pa.
Wagner, Mrs. S. C............................Newville, Pa.
Wagner, Mrs. Sue.......................Green Spring, Pa.
Wallace, Mrs. W. L..........................Newville, Pa.
Watkins, Mrs. H. J........................... " "
Weary, Mrs. H. N..................................Allen, Pa.
Westafer, Miss Jennie................Green Spring, Pa.
Wheeler, Mrs. Anna.........................Newville, Pa.
Wiest, Miss Aggie............................... " "
Wiest, Mrs. Geo..............................Centreville, Pa.
Wiestling, Mrs. Dr. R. R................Huntingdon, Pa.
Wild, Mrs. S. G....................................Moline, Ill.
Williams, Mrs. Kate E.................Green Spring, Pa.
Williams, Mrs. Lottie.......................Newville, Pa.
Woodburn, Mrs. Col........................ " "
Woodburn, Miss Nellie....................... " "

RECIPES.

MARBLE CAKES.

1. White Part.—1½ cups white sugar, ½ cup butter, ½ cup sweet milk, ½ teaspoon soda, 1 teaspoon cream tartar, whites of 4 eggs.
Dark Part.—2 cups brown sugar, ½ cup butter, ½ cup sour milk, 1 teaspoon cream tartar, ½ teaspoon soda, 2½ cups flour, yolks of 4 eggs, cloves, cinnamon, and nutmeg.

2. White Part.—Whites of 4 eggs, 1 cup white sugar, ½ cup butter, ½ cup sweet milk, 1 teaspoon cream tartar, ½ do. soda.
Dark Part.—Yolks of 4 eggs, 1 cup brown sugar, ½ cup molasses, ½ cup butter, ½ cup sour milk, 1 teaspoon soda, plenty of all kinds of spices such as suit the taste.

3. White Part.—2 cups white sugar, 1 cup butter, 1 cup sour cream, 1 teaspoon soda, the whites of 7 eggs, 3 cups flour, flavor with lemon.
Dark Part.—1 cup molasses, 2 cups brown sugar, 1 cup butter, the yolks of 7 eggs, 2 teaspoons cinnamon, 1 teaspoon cloves, 1 teaspoon allspice, 1 teaspoon black pepper, 1 grated nutmeg, 1 cup sour cream, 1 teaspoon soda, 5 cups flour, mix this by itself.

4. White Part.—2 cups white sugar, 1 cup butter, 1 cup milk, 1 teaspoon soda, 2 teaspoons cream tartar, 3½ cups flour, whites of 7 eggs beaten to a stiff froth.
Dark Part.—3 cups brown sugar, 1 cup molasses, 1 cup cream, 1 cup butter, 1 tablespoon cloves, 1 tablespoon cinnamon, 1 nutmeg, 1 teaspoon pepper, 1 teaspoon soda, yolks of 7 eggs, 4 cups flour.

5. Light Part.—1½ cups white sugar, ½ cup butter, ½ cup sour milk, ½ teaspoon soda, 1 teaspoon cream tartar, the whites of 4 eggs, 2½ cups flour.
Dark Part.—1 cup brown sugar, ½ cup sour milk, ½ cup butter, ½ teaspoon soda, 1 do. cream tartar, 2½ cups flour, yolks of 4 eggs, cloves, allspice, cinnamon, nutmeg. Bake 1 hour.

6. White Part.—Whites of 5 eggs, 1 cup white sugar, ½ cup butter, ½ cup sweet cream, ½ teaspoon soda, 1 teaspoon cream tartar.
Dark Part.—Yolks of 5 eggs, 1 cup brown sugar, ½ cup molasses, ½ cup butter, ½ cup sour cream, 1 teaspoon of soda, 1 teaspoon cloves, 1 teaspoon cinnamon, a little nutmeg and flour to make it pretty stiff, first dark in the pan, then white, then dark, then white, etc.

7. White Part.—1 cup sweet milk, 1 do. butter, 3 do. white sugar, 4 cups flour, whites of 8 eggs, ½ teaspoon saleratus, 1 teaspoon of cream tartar, flavor with lemon.

Dark Part.—1 cup butter, 1 cup sweet milk, 3 cups brown sugar, 1 cup molasses, 5 cups flour, yolks of 8 eggs and whole of another, 1 teaspoon of saleratus, 2 teaspoons cream tartar, 2 tablespoons cinnamon, 1 tablespoon cloves, 1 tablespoon allspice, 1 nutmeg, 1 teaspoon pepper, first put in a layer of dark, then the white, and so on until the loaf is completed.

8. White Part.—1½ cups flour, 1 cup white sugar, not quite ½ cup sweet milk, the whites of 6 eggs, ½ teaspoon cream tartar, ¼ teaspoon soda, ¼ cup butter.

Dark Part.—1½ cups flour, 1 cup very dark sugar, not quite ½ cup sweet milk, the yolks of 6 eggs, ½ teaspoon cream tartar, ¼ teaspoon soda, ¼ cup butter.

FRUIT CAKES.

1. 1 dozen eggs, 2 pounds raisins, 2 pounds currants, 1 pound citron, little over 1 pound flour, 1 pound butter, 1 pound sugar, beat butter and flour together, beat sugar and yolks of eggs together, and pour into the butter and flour, beat the white of eggs well, and pour into butter, sugar and flour. Flour your fruit *well*, put in citron, and mix with the rest.

2. 1 pound butter, 1 pound currants, 1 pound dark brown sugar, 1 pound flour, ¼ pound citron, 10 eggs, 3 pounds raisins, ½ ounce mace, 1 teaspoon soda, 1 tablespoon cinnamon, 1 tablespoon cloves, 1 gill brandy, bake steady 4 hours.

3. 3 cups brown sugar, 2 cups butter, 1½ cups buttermilk, 1 teaspoon soda, 4 eggs, 2 teaspoons baking powder, 1 pound raisins, 1 pounds currants, 1 pound citron, 1 teaspoon ground cloves, 1 teaspoon ground cinnamon, 1 teaspoon allspice, 5 cups flour, put the fruit in at last.

4. 1 pound sugar, 1 pound flour, 1 pound butter, 10 eggs, 1 cup molasses, soda to make it foam, 5 pounds fruit, 1 pound citron, 1 glass brandy, 2 glasses wine, cloves, cinnamon, mace, bake six hours in a slow oven. This is excellent.

5. 1 pound sugar, 1 pound butter, ¼ pound wheat flour, 1 dozen eggs, 2 pounds raisins, 2 pounds currants, ¼ pound citron, 1 cup molasses, ginger, cloves, etc., to the taste.

6. 5 eggs, 2 cups sugar, ½ lb. French currants, ½ lb. raisins, 1 cup strong coffee, 1 teaspoon each ground nutmegs and cloves, 1 teaspoon of soda dissolved in 1 tablespoon vinegar, 3½ cups flour.

7. 1 cup cold strong coffee, 1½ cups brown sugar, ⅔ cup butter, 1 cup molasses, 1 cup raisins, 1 tablespoon soda, nutmeg, cinnamon, and citron.

8. 2 eggs, 1 cup butter, 1 cup sugar, 1 cup molasses, 1 cup strong coffee (made), 1 tablespoon spoon soda, 1 pound raisins, chopped fine; add cinnamon, nutmegs and cloves to taste. Do not make too stiff. Bake in a moderate oven.

9. 1 lb. white sugar, ¾ lb. butter, 1 lb. sifted flour, 2 lbs. raisins, 2 lbs. currants, 1 dozen eggs, ½ lb. citron, 1 teaspoon cinnamon, 1 teaspoon cloves, 1 nutmeg, 1 glass wine, 1 glass brandy, mix butter and sugar together, then yolks of eggs and part of the flour, spices, the whites of eggs well beaten, the remainder of flour, lastly fruit.

Hard icing, (good).—Mix sugar and eggs together before beating.

10. 1 lb. white sugar, 1 do. flour, ½ do. butter, 6 eggs, 1 cup thick milk, 1 qt. hickory-nut kernels, 1 lb. currants, 1 lb. raisins, 1 teaspoon soda in hot water, 1 tablespoon cinnamon, 1 do. cloves, 1 do. nutmeg.

11. 1 lb. butter, 1 do. white sugar, 1 doz. eggs, 1 lb. flour, 2 lbs. raisins, 2 do. currants, ½ do. citron, 1 tablespoon mace, 2 do. cloves, 1 do. cinnamon, 1 do. nutmeg, 1 do. allspice.

12. Take ½ cup molasses, 6 cups flour, 3 cups sugar, 2 cups butter, 1 cup milk, 5 eggs, 2 nutmegs, 2 teaspoons cloves powdered, 2 teaspoons ground allspice, 2 teaspoons ground cinnamon, about ¼ ounce mace, 1 wineglass brandy, 2 lbs. currants, 2 lbs. raisins, 1 teaspoon soda, bake carefully in a well-heated oven.

13. 1 pt. light dough, 1 cup sugar, 1 cup butter, 3 eggs, 1 teaspoon saleratus, 1 lb. raisins, nutmeg or cinnamon to the taste. Bake 1 hour. Let it stand and rise a little before baking.

14. 2 cups brown sugar, 2 do. molasses, 1½ cups butter, 1 do. milk, 1½ cups currants, ½ do. citron, 6 cups flour, 1 tablespoon cloves, 1 do. cinnamon, 1 nutmeg, ½ teaspoon soda, 5 eggs.

15. 1½ cups molasses, 1 do. sugar, 1½ cups butter, 6 do. flour, 3 eggs, 2 lbs. raisins, ½ do. citron, 1 do. currants, 1 teaspoon cloves, 1 do. cinnamon, 1 do. soda, 1 cup of sour milk. Stir well, bake 2 hours. Mix the fruit with the flour and stir in last.—*Cousin's Cake.*

16. 3 cups brown sugar, 2 do. butter, 1½ do. sweet milk, 5 do. flour, 4 eggs, 2 teaspoons baking powder, 1 lb. raisins, 1 do. currants, 1 tablespoon cinnamon, 1 do. cloves, 1 do. allspice.

17. Dry and sift 4 lbs. flour, 4 do. butter with the salt washed out, 2 do. loaf sugar, 1 oz. nutmeg, 1 do. mace pounded, wash 4 lbs. currants dry, pick, and rub them in flour, stone and cut 2 lbs. raisins, slice 2 lbs. citron, blanch 1 lb. sweet almonds and cut them in slices, 30 eggs, work butter with your hands until it creams. Put in alternately the flour, sugar and eggs; when all are in and the cake looks like light, add the spice, fruit, almonds and half pint brandy. Half the quantity makes two nice cakes. Bake three hours.

18. Dry and sift 4 lbs. flour, 4 do. butter, 2 do. sugar, 1 oz. nutmeg, 1 do. mace, 1 lb. currants, 2 do. raisins, 2 do. citron, 1 lb. almonds, 30 eggs, ½ pint brandy.

19. 2 cups sugar, 1 do. molasses, 1½ cups butter, 6 eggs, 1 lb. raisins, 1 do. currants, spice to taste.

POUND CAKES.

1. 10 eggs, 1 lb. sugar, 1 do. butter, flour to stiffen.

2. 1 cup sugar, 1 do. molasses, 1 do. sweet cream, 1 tablespoon soda, 4 cups flour, 1 cup lard, 4 eggs, stir all together without beating the eggs.

3. 3 eggs, 2 cups sugar, ½ do. butter, 1 do. cold water, 3 do. flour, 1 teaspoon cream tartar, 1 do. soda, nutmeg.

4. 4 cups flour, 2 do. sugar, 1 do. butter, 1 do. sour cream, 3 eggs, ½ teaspoon soda.

5. ¾ lb. butter, 1 do. white sugar, 1 do. flour, 10 eggs, flavored with a little lemon.

6. 1 lb. sugar, 1 do. flour, 1½ do. butter, 1 teaspoonful soda, 2 do. cream tartar, 1 cup sour milk, 5 eggs, vanilla.

7. 1 cup butter, 3 do. sugar, 1 do. water or milk, 4 do. flour, 6 eggs, 1 teaspoon soda, 2 do. cream tartar.

8. 8 eggs beaten well, 1 lb. sugar, 1 do. flour, 1 do. butter, 1 teaspoon baking powder.

9. 1 lb. sugar, ½ do. flour, ½ do. cornstarch, ¾ do. butter, whites of 19 eggs, rosewater, brandy and lemon. This is a superior cake.

10. 3 cups flour, 1 do. butter, 2 do. sugar, whites of 6 eggs, ½ teaspoon soda, 1 do. cream tartar, 1 cup milk, grate 1 small cocoanut, and put in two-thirds of it last.

SPONGE CAKES.

1. 1 cup sugar, 1 do. flour, 3 eggs, whites beaten separately, 1 teaspoon cream tartar, ¼ teaspoon soda dissolved in 1 tablespoon of hot water.

2. 2 cups sugar, 2 cups flour, 6 eggs.

3. 3 eggs, 1 cup sugar, 1 do. flour. Beat the eggs very light, then put in the sugar, stir in the flour, 1 tablespoon milk with a little soda or baking powder, and flavor to taste.

4. 1 tumbler sugar, 1 do. flour, 1 do. water, 2 eggs, ½ teaspoon soda.

5. 1 cup sugar, 1 do. flour, 3 eggs, 1 teaspoon cream tartar, teaspoon three parts full of soda, dissolved in a bit of milk.

6. 1 cup white sugar, 2 tablespoons butter, 1 cup sweet milk, 1 teaspoon soda, 1 tin cup flour, 1 egg, and nutmeg to taste.

7. 1 lb. sugar, 10 eggs, 10 oz. flour, season with nutmeg, stir the yolks and sugar together. Beat the whites thoroughly, mix, add the flour, and bake immediately.

8. 1 cup flour, 1 tablespoon butter, 1 cup sugar, 3 eggs, 1 tablespoon sweet milk.

9. 10 eggs, 1 tin cup flour, 1 lb. sugar.

10. 4 eggs well beaten, 2 cups sugar, 1 cup flour beaten into $\frac{1}{2}$ cup cold water, 1$\frac{1}{2}$ cups flour, 2 teaspoons yeast powder.

11. 1 cup sugar, 2 eggs, 1$\frac{1}{2}$ cups flour, $\frac{3}{4}$ do. water, 1 teaspoon baking powder, and flavor with lemon.

12. 1 lb. sugar, 1 doz. eggs, 1 pt. flour, 1 nutmeg. Separate the eggs, beat the whites until stiff, then add the sugar and beat well, then the yolks, and lastly the flour, stirring in lightly.

13. 2 cups sugar, 2 do. flour, 4 eggs, $\frac{1}{2}$ cup cold water, 2 teaspoons baking powder, beat the whites to a stiff froth and add the last thing, beat water and yolks together.

14. 2 cups sugar, 2 do. flour, 4 eggs beaten very light, $\frac{1}{2}$ cup cold water, 2 teaspoons baking powder, 1 do. vanilla, a little salt.

15. 4 eggs, 1$\frac{1}{2}$ cups sugar, beaten together until you can get it no lighter, add flour enough to thicken; the beating of the eggs and sugar is what makes this cake.

16. 4 eggs, 2 cups sugar, 2 do. flour, $\frac{3}{4}$ cup of hot water, 1 teaspoon soda, 2 do. cream tartar, $\frac{1}{2}$ do. vanilla.

17. 1 teacup sweet cream, 4 eggs beaten separately, 3 cups flour, 2 cups sugar, 1 teaspoon soda and 2 of cream tartar.

18. 8 eggs, 1 tin cup sugar beaten light, 1 tablespoon vinegar, 1 tin cup flour. Bake slowly.

19. 9 eggs, 1 tin cup sugar, 1 tin cup flour.

CORN-STARCH CAKES.

1. 1 cup butter, 2 do sugar, 1 do. sweet milk, the whites of 7 eggs, 2 cups flour, 1 do. corn starch, 2 teaspoons cream tartar, 1 do. soda.

2. 1 cup butter, 2 do. sugar, 1 do. corn starch, 1 do. flour, the whites of 7 eggs, 1 cup sweet milk, 1$\frac{1}{2}$ teaspoons baking powder.

3. Whites of 6 eggs, 2 cups sugar, 1 do. butter, 2 do. flour, 1 do. corn starch, 2 do. sweet milk, 2 teaspoons baking powder in the flour and sifted, flavor with lemon. Bake as soon as mixed.

4. 1$\frac{1}{2}$ cups sugar, $\frac{1}{2}$ do. butter, 1 do. flour, a little more than a cup corn starch, $\frac{1}{2}$ do. sour milk, whites of 3 eggs, very little soda, teaspoon extract lemon.

5. 3 cups white sugar, 1 do. butter, 1 do. sweet milk, 1 do. corn starch, 3 do. flour, 3 teaspoons baking powder, whites of 12 eggs, beat the butter to a cream, then add the sugar, milk and baking powder, then the corn starch, the whites of eggs and flour being the last; the eggs should be beaten to a stiff froth.

6. 2 eggs, 1 tablespoon butter, 2 cups sugar, 2 tablespoons corn starch, put in 1 cup milk to thicken, and 2 teaspoons yeast powder.

7. ¾ cup butter, 2 do. sugar, 1 do. sweet milk, 2 do. flour, 1 do. corn starch, ½ teaspoon soda, 1 do. cream tartar, whites of 6 eggs.

8. 1 lb. sugar, 7 eggs, whites, 1 cup butter, 1 do. sweet milk, 2 teaspoons baking powder, 1 cup corn starch, 3 cups flour, flavor with lemon.

JELLY CAKES.

1. 6 eggs, 3 cups sugar, 1 do. sweet cream, 1 do. butter, 1 teaspoon soda, 2 do. cream tartar, 5 cups flour.

2. 1 egg, 2½ cups flour, 1 do. sugar, 1 do. milk, butter the size of a walnut, 1 teaspoon soda, 1 do. cream tartar.

3. Whites and yolks of 6 eggs, 3 cups sugar, 4 teaspoons yeast powder, 2 cups butter, ¾ do. milk, flour enough to make a batter, beat eggs, sugar and butter together, then put in flour and yeast powder, mix well, then add milk, and flavor to taste.

4. 1 lb. sugar, 4 eggs, ¾ cup butter, 3 do. flour, 1 do. sour cream, 1 teaspoon soda, 2 do. cream tartar.

5. 3 cups sugar, 4 eggs, ½ pt. sour cream, 1 teaspoon soda or sweet cream, 2 do. cream tartar, add a little butter.

6. 2 cups sugar, 1 do. butter, 3 do. flour, 1 do. sweet milk, 1 teaspoon saleratus, and 2 do. cream tartar, to be mixed in the flour.

7. Whites of 4 eggs, 1 cup sugar, ½ do. butter, ½ do. sour cream, teaspoon soda, 1 do. cream tartar, nearly 2 cups flour, spice to taste.

8. 1 cup sugar, yolks of 4 eggs, ½ cup butter, ½ do. sour cream, add 2 tablespoons thick milk to the cream, 1 teaspoon soda, 1 do. cream tartar, nearly 2 cups flour.

9. 1 cup sour milk, 2 do. sugar, 3 eggs, lump of butter the size of a walnut, 2 teaspoons cream tartar, 1 do. soda.

10. 1 lb. sugar, 4 cups flour, 6 eggs, 1 cup butter, 1 do. cream, 1 teaspoon soda, 2 do. cream tartar, spice to taste.

11. 3 eggs, 2 cups sugar, 3½ do. flour, 1 do. butter, 1 do. sweet milk, 1 teaspoon soda, 1 do. cream tartar.

12. 2 cups sugar, 3 do. flour, 4 eggs, a lump of butter the size of a walnut, 1 teaspoon soda, 1 do. cream tartar, and thin it with buttermilk.

13. 1 lb. sugar, 6 eggs, 1 cup butter, 1 do. sour cream, 1 teaspoon soda, 2 do. cream tartar, 3½ cups flour, flavor with lemon, bake in a quick oven. Splendid.

14. 1 cup butter, 4 eggs, 2 cups sugar, 1 do. sour milk, 3 do. flour, 1 teaspoon soda.

15. 4 cups flour, 4 eggs, 2 cups sugar, 2 teaspoons cream tartar, 1 do. soda, ½ tin cup sweet cream, a little butter, beat the yolks of the eggs and sugar together, stir in the cream and flour, and add the other ingredients.

16. 2 cups sugar, 2 eggs, 1 cup butter, ½ do. sour milk, 3 do. flour, 1 teaspoon soda, 2 do. cream tartar, put the cream tartar in the flour dry.

17. 3 cups sugar, 4 eggs, 4 cups flour, ½ pt. sour cream, 2 teaspoons cream tartar, 1 do. soda, lump of butter the size of a walnut, beat whites of eggs separate, beat the yolks and sugar together, stir in cream, and add the other ingredients.

18. 3 eggs, ½ cup white sugar, 1 do. flour, 1 teaspoon soda or cream tartar, 1½ do. baking powder, bake in thin cakes, spread with jelly, and roll up with the jelly side in, and cut in slices across the roll.

19. 1 tumbler flour, 2 teaspoons baking powder, sift the flour and powder together, 1 tea cup sugar, 3 eggs, 2 tablespoons water, beat eggs and sugar together, add the water, then the flour. Bake in jelly pans.

Cream Jelly.—1 pt. sweet milk, let it come to a boil, then add a piece of butter size of hulled walnut, 2 tablespoons sugar, 1 do. extract of lemon, 2 do. corn starch dissolved in milk, put in while the milk is boiling, when boiled a few minutes take off, and when cool spread over the layers.

20. 3 eggs, 1 cup sugar, 1 teaspoon cream tartar, ½ do. soda, 1 cup flour, pour into long pans, and bake. When done, spread jelly on the bottom, roll up, and when cold cut in slices.

21. 12 eggs, 1 lb. sugar, the weight of 6 eggs in flour, run out in pans, jelly while warm and roll.

22. 1 cup butter, 2 do. sugar, 3 do. flour, 4 eggs, 1 teaspoon soda, ½ cup sour cream.

CREAM AND CUSTARD CAKES.

1. 1 cup sugar, 2 tablespoons melted butter, ⅔ cup sweet milk, 2 teaspoons baking powder, 2 cups flour, whites of 3 eggs beaten very light, bake in 3 layers in jelly rings.

Custard for putting cake together.—½ pt. sweet cream, yolk of 1 egg, 1 teaspoon corn starch, 2 tablespoons sugar, 1 teaspoon lemon, mix well, boil a few minutes, stir well all the time, spread it on the cakes and put together.

2. 3 eggs, 1 cup sugar, 1 do. flour, 2 tablespoons water, 1 teaspoon cream tartar, 1 do. soda, bake in a long pan, split while warm and spread with the following cream, and put together as they were when they came out of the oven.

To make the cream.—1 scant pt. sweet milk, 1 tablespoon corn starch, 2 eggs, ½ cup sugar, and 1 teaspoon vanilla.

3. 1 cup sour cream, 2 do. sugar, 3 do. flour, 4 eggs, 1 tablespoon soda, 2 teaspoons cream tartar in flour.

4. 1 cup sour cream, 1 do. sweet cream, 2 do. sugar, 4 eggs, 1 tablespoon soda, 1 cup butter, and flour to make stiff as a sponge cake.

5. 1 cup sugar, 1 egg, butter half the size of an egg, 1 cup sweet milk, 3 do. flour, 1 teaspoon soda, 2 do. cream tartar, or 3 do. baking powder.
    Custard for cake.— 1 egg; 3 teaspoons flour, 1 cup milk, 2 tablespoons white sugar, mixed and boiled to a custard, flavor the cake and also the custard, with lemon, and use the custard as a jelly between the layers of the cake.

6. Yolks of 10 eggs, 1 pound sugar, 1 cup rich sour cream, 1 cup corn starch, 1½ cups flour, 2 teaspoons cream tartar, 1 teaspoon soda, essence of lemon to taste, icing made of whites of 7 eggs, 1 lb. of powdered sugar, 1 large box of cocoanut.

7. 4 cups flour, 2 cups sugar, 3 cups cream, 4 eggs, 1 teaspoon soda. Bake well.

8. 1 cup sugar, 1 cup sour cream, 2 cups of flour, 1 teaspoon soda, 1 of cream tartar, and 3 eggs.

COCOANUT CAKES.

1. ½ cup butter, 3 do. sugar, 4 do. flour, 5 eggs, 1 cup sweet milk, 1 teaspoon soda, 1 do. cream tartar, 1 cocoanut.

2. 1 cup white sugar, 1 do. sweet milk, ½ do. butter, 3 do. flour, the yolks of 4 eggs, beat the sugar and butter together, then add the yolks, when well beaten, and milk, 2 teaspoons baking powder, bake on pie tins the same as for jelly cake, take the whites and beat to a stiff froth, add white sugar so as to make frosting, then take of the prepared cocoanut, and when the cakes are baked, spread over a layer of cocoanut, then the frosting the same as jelly cake.

3. 1 cup butter, 3 do. sugar, 1 do. milk, 4½ do. flour, 4 eggs, 1 teaspoon soda, 2 do. cream tartar, and 1 grated cocoanut.

4. 2 cups sugar, ¾ cup butter, 1 do. sour milk, 4 eggs, 1 teaspoon soda, 1 do. cream tartar, 4 cups flour, 1 grated cocoanut, bake in jelly moulds.

5. 2 cups powdered sugar, ½ do. butter, 3 eggs, 1 cup milk, 3 cups flour, 2 teaspoons cream tartar, 1 do. soda.

6. 1 lb. butter, 2 do. sugar, 2 grated cocoanuts mixed well, 1 cup milk and milk of the cocoanuts, 1¾ lbs. flour, 10 eggs, nutmeg if desired, ½ teaspoon soda. This quantity makes 2 cakes.

7. 1 cup butter, 3 do. sugar, 4 do. flour, 1 do. sweet milk, 5 eggs, 1 teaspoon soda, 2 do. cream tarter, 1 grated cocoanut, put half of it in the batter, ice the cake and sprinkle the remaining half on the icing while moist.

8. 5 eggs, whites beaten separately, 3 cups sugar, 1 do. sour cream, 1 do. butter, 4½ do. flour, the milk of the nut and half the grated nut in the cake, the other half in the icing, with ½ lb. icing sugar.

9. 1 grated cocoanut, 1 lb. refined sugar, ½ lb. butter, 1 lb. flour, 3 eggs, roll thin and bake in a quick oven.

10. 1 lb. flour, 1 do. sugar, ½ lb. butter, 6 eggs, 1 grated cocoanut, beat eggs separate, cream the butter, then add in sugar, beat very light, then mix alternately, flour, eggs and cocoanut. Bake one hour.

11. Beat the whites of 8 eggs to a froth, 2 cups sugar, ⅔ cup butter, ¾ do. sweet milk, 2 cups flour, 2½ teaspoons yeast powder.
Icing.—Take the whites of 2 eggs, 4 tablespoons sugar, spread this on the cake and then sprinkle the cocoanut.

12. The whites of 8 eggs, grate a good sized cocoanut the night before you want to use it, bake the cake in jelly cake pans, when it is cooling make an icing of whites of 4 eggs, 1 lb. of fine pulverized sugar, spread each layer of the cake with the icing and on the icing spread the cocoanut. Ice the cake on the top and on sides, put a layer of grated cocoanut over all the icing.

CHOCOLATE CAKES.

1. 1 lb. sand sugar, ½ lb. butter, 1 lb. flour, 6 eggs, 2 teaspoons cream tartar, 1 teaspoon soda dissolved in ½ pt. sweet milk, the grated rind and juice of 1 lemon, beat the butter and sugar to a cream, then add the yolks well beaten, then the milk, and last the whites. Bake in thin layers.
Icing.—1 cake chocolate, the whites of six eggs, 1½ lbs. sugar, a little cream, beat the eggs as for icing, add the sugar and chocolate, which must be grated, and add the cream.

2. 2 eggs, 1 cup sugar, ½ do. butter, ½ do. milk, 2 do. flour, 2 teaspoons baking powder, flavoring. This makes three layers.
For Custard.—½ cake sweet chocolate, grated, pour on enough boiling water to dissolve it, stir into this the white of an egg, 1 tablespoon flour, 2 do. milk, ½ cup sugar, and boil until quite thick.

3. 2 cups sugar, 1 do. butter, 1 do. milk, 3½ do. flour, ½ nutmeg, ½ teaspoon soda, 1 do. cream tartar, yolks of 5 eggs, whites of 3 eggs, beating the remaining 3 whites to a stiff froth with ½ cup sugar and 5 teaspoons chocolate, to make the icing.

SILVER AND GOLD CAKES.

1. Whites of 12 eggs, beaten to a stiff froth, 5 cups flour, 3 do. sugar, 1 do. butter, ½ do. cream, 1 teaspoon cream tartar, ½ do. soda.

2. Whites of 12 eggs, 5 cups flour, 1 cup white sugar, 1 do. butter, 1 do. cream or sweet milk, 1 teaspoon cream tartar, ½ do. soda, beat and mix as gold cake, and bake in a deep pan.

3. 2 cups sugar, ½ do. butter, ¼ do. milk, ½ teaspoon soda, 1 do. cream tartar, the whites of 8 eggs, ¾ cup flour.

4. Whites of 8 eggs, 2 cups sugar, 2¼ do. flour, ½ do. butter, ½ do. milk, ½ teaspoon soda, ½ do. cream tartar, flavor with almonds, sift cream tartar and flour.

5. 1 lb. sugar, 1 lb. butter, 1 cup thick milk, the yolks of 8 eggs for the gold, taking the whites for the silver; 1 teaspoon soda for each, 1 teaspoon cream tartar, 4 cups flour.

6. Yolks of 12 eggs, 5 cups flour, 3 do. sugar, 1 do. butter, ½ do. cream, 1 teaspoon cream tartar, 1 do. soda.

7. Yolks of 12 eggs, 5 cups flour, 3 do. white sugar, 1 do. butter, 1½ do. cream or sweet milk, ½ teaspoon soda, 1 do. cream tartar, bake in a deep loaf pan, when each part is ready, drop a spoon of the silver, then a spoon of the gold over the bottom of the dish in which it is to be baked, and so proceed to fill up the pan, dropping one upon the other with the different layers, and it will give you still another variety from the gold and silver cake.

8. Yolks of 8 eggs, ½ cup sugar, ½ do. butter, 2 do. flour, ½ do. milk, ½ teaspoon soda, 1 do. cream tartar, flavor with rose, bake in hot oven.

9. Yolks of 11 eggs, beaten; 2 cups sugar, 1 cup milk, 1 cup butter, 4 cups flour, 4 teaspoons baking powder.

10. 1½ cups sugar, whites of 10 eggs, 1 teaspoon cream tartar.

11. 2 cups sugar, ½ cup butter, yolks of 10 eggs, 1 teaspoon soda, 1 do. cream tartar, 1 cup sour cream, 3 cups flour.

DELICATE CAKES.

1. 2 cups sugar, ¾ do. butter, 1 do. sweet milk, 1 do. cornstarch, ½ teaspoon soda mixed in the milk, 1 do. cream tartar mixed in 2 cups flour, whites of 7 eggs beat to a stiff froth, add eggs last and flavor with lemon or vanilla.

2. Beat together 1 cup butter and 2 do. sugar, then add 1 do. sweet milk, beat the whites of 8 eggs to a froth, ¾ lb. flour, 1 teaspoon soda, 2 do. cream tartar sifted through the flour, and flavor with vanilla.

3. 1 lb. powdered sugar, ¾ lb. flour, 6 oz. butter, whites of 14 eggs beaten to a stiff froth, mace or bitter almonds, grated; bake in flat tins from half to three-quarters of an hour.

4. 1 lb. sugar, whites of 7 eggs, 1 cup butter, 1 do. sweet milk, 4 do. flour, and 3 teaspoons baking powder.

5. 1 cup butter, 2 do. sugar, 3 do. flour, 1 do. milk, whites of 6 eggs, 1 teaspoon cream tartar, flavor with vanilla.

FEATHER CAKES.

1. 1 cup sugar, 1½ do. flour, ⅔ do. sweet milk, 1 egg, 1 teaspoon butter, 3 do. baking powder.

2. *Kate's Feather Cake.*—1 cup sugar, 1 do. milk, 1 teaspoon butter, 1 egg, 2½ cups flour, 2 teaspoons cream tartar, 1 do. soda, and flavor to taste with nutmeg or lemon.

3. 3 cups sugar, 1 cup butter, 3 cups flour, ¾ cup corn starch, 1 cup water, 5 eggs, 3 teaspoons baking powder. Bake in pans.

CUP CAKES.

1. 4 eggs, 2 cups sugar, 1 cup butter, 1 cup sweet milk, 1 cup corn starch, 1 teaspoon soda, 1 teaspoon cream tartar mixed in 2 cups flour, spice or flavor to taste, bake in jelly-cake pans, and ice with frosting when cold.

2. 2 cups flour, 1 cup sweet milk, 1 cup butter, 3 cups flour, 3 eggs, 1 teaspoon cream tartar, 1 teaspoon soda.

3. 2 cups sugar, 4 eggs, 1 cup thick milk, 1 cup butter, 4 cups flour, 1 teaspoon soda, 2 teaspoons cream tartar, pour in pans and bake.

4. 1 cup butter, 2 cups sugar, 4 eggs, 3 cups flour, 1 teaspoon baking powder.

5. 2 cups sugar, ½ cup sweet milk, ½ cup butter, 3 eggs, 3½ cups flour, 2 teaspoons baking powder, and flavor to taste.

6. 1 cup butter, 1 cup molasses, 1 cup sugar, 4 cups flour, 1 cup cream tartar, 1 teaspoon soda, 1 tablespoon ginger and cloves, 5 eggs, beat until light, fill your cups half full.

7. 3 cups flour, 3 eggs, 2 cups sugar, 1 cup milk, 1 teaspoon soda, 2 teaspoons cream tartar, half gill wine, and nutmeg.

8. 2 cups sugar, 3 cups flour, 1 cup butter, 1 cup sweet milk, ½ teaspoon soda, 1 teaspoon cream tartar, 5 eggs.

NUT CAKES.

1. 3 eggs, 2 cups sugar, 3 cups flour, 1 cup sweet milk, ½ cup butter, 1½ teaspoons cream tartar, 1 teaspoon soda, 1 pint hickory-nut kernels, 1 lb. raisins, mix sugar and butter, beat whites of eggs separately, take 1 teaspoon flour and mix with the raisins and kernels.

2. 2 cups sugar, 2 cups butter, 1 cup milk, 1 teaspoon soda, 2 teaspoons cream tartar, 3½ cups flour, 2 cups hickory-nut kernels.

3. 1 lb. hickory-nut kernels, 1 lb. sugar, whites of 6 eggs, beat the sugar and eggs together until light.

4. 1 cup butter, 2 cups sugar, 4 eggs beaten separately, 1 cup buttermilk, 1 qt. flour, ¾ teaspoon soda dissolved in the milk, ¾ lb. raisins, 1½ pts. hickory-nut kernels, 1 wine glass brandy, and bake one hour and a half.

"MOUNTAIN" CAKES.

1. 1 lb. sugar, 1 cup butter, ½ cup sweet milk, whites of 10 eggs, 3½ cups flour, 1 teaspoon cream tartar, ½ teaspoon soda, bake in 3 jelly-cake pans. When perfectly cold, make an icing of the whites of 3 eggs, and spread it on the same as jelly.

2. The whites of 7 eggs, 2 cups sugar, ½ cup butter, ⅔ cup sweet milk, 3 cups flour, 1 teaspoon soda, 2 teaspoons cream tartar, bake in jelly pans.
For Icing.—The whites of 3 eggs and 1 lb. sugar.

3. 1 lb. sugar, 1 cup butter, beaten to a cream, break in 6 eggs, two at a time, ½ cup sour cream, ½ cup sour milk, mixed, ½ teaspoon soda mixed in half the milk, 1 teaspoon cream tartar in the other half, 1 lb. flour, and flavor to taste.

4. 1 cup butter, 3 cups sugar, cream them, ½ cup sweet milk, teaspoon cream tartar, put in the milk, ½ teaspoon soda in 3½ cups flour, the whites of 10 eggs, beat very light, the flour last in small quantities, bake in three cakes. Make an icing of 3 eggs to 1 lb. pulverized sugar, and flavor with lemon.

5. ½ cup butter, 3 cups white sugar, cream together, 1 cup sweet milk, 1 teaspoon cream tartar, little more than ½ teaspoon soda, 4 cups flour, 10 eggs beaten very lightly, and add eggs and flour beaten very lightly.

6. 1 cup sour cream, 2 cups white sugar, 3½ cups flour, 1 cup butter, whites of 5 eggs, 1 teaspoon soda, 1 teaspoon cream tartar.

7. 1 cup sweet milk, whites of 10 eggs, 4 cups flour, 1 cup butter, 2 cups sugar, 2 teaspoons cream tartar, 1 teaspoon soda. Put icing between layers.

8. 1 cup sugar, ½ cup butter, ½ cup milk, ½ cup flour, 2 eggs, 1 teaspoon cream tartar, ½ teaspoon soda, and flavor with nutmeg.

9. 3 cups sugar, 1½ cups sour cream, 5 eggs, 3½ cups flour, 1 teaspoon butter, 2 teaspoons cream tartar, and 1 teaspoon soda.

10. 1 lb. sugar, 1 cup butter beaten to cream, ½ cup sweet milk, 3 cups flour, ½ teaspoon soda, 1 teaspoon cream tartar, whites 10 eggs, or 5 whole eggs, flavor with vanilla. Bake in layers. Icing made of whites of 3 eggs to 1 lb. of powdered sugar, and flavor with rosewater.

11. 2 cups sugar, ⅔ cup butter, whites of 7 eggs well beaten, ⅔ cup sweet milk, 2 cups flour, 1 do. corn starch, 2 teaspoons baking powder. Bake in jelly tins.
Frosting.—Whites of 3 eggs and sugar beaten together, not quite as stiff as usual for frosting; spread over the cake, and some grated cocoanut, then put the cake together; put cocoanut or frosting on top.

12. 4 eggs, whites, 2 cups white sugar, ½ cup beaten lard, 1 cup sour milk, 1 teaspoon soda, 2 teaspoons cream tartar, 3 cups flour; bake like jelly cake.

13. 2 cups sugar, 1 do. butter, whites of 6 eggs, ½ cup sweet milk, 3 cups flour, 1 teaspoon soda, 2 do. cream tartar; bake like jelly cake; put icing between.
Icing.—½ lb. sugar, whites 3 eggs.

14. Whites 12 eggs, 3 cups sugar, 1 cup butter, do. sour milk, 2 teaspoons cream tartar, 1 do. soda, 3 cups flour, 1 cup corn starch.

SUGAR CAKES.

1. 3 cups sugar, 1 cup lard or butter, 3 eggs, 1 cup sweet milk, 1 teaspoon soda, 2 teaspoons cream tartar, make up as soft as can be rolled.

2. 1 lb. sugar, 3 eggs, 1 cup sour milk, 1 teaspoon soda, 1 cup shortening.

3. 1 lb. sugar, 3 eggs, 1 cup shortening, ½ cup milk, 1 teaspoon soda, 1 teaspoon cream tartar.

4. 1 lb. sugar, ½ lb. butter, 2 eggs, 1 teaspoon soda dissolved in 1 cup thick cream, 1 nutmeg.

5. 2 cups sugar, 1 cup butter, 1 cup sour cream, 2 eggs, flour to stiffen, bake in a quick oven.

6. 1 lb. sugar, 4 eggs, 1 cup butter, 1 cup milk, 1 teaspoon cream tartar.

7. 1 lb. sugar, 1 tumbler buttermilk, ½ cup butter, 1 teaspoon soda, 1 teaspoon pulverized alum, and 3 eggs.

8. 1 lb. white sugar, 4 eggs, 1 cup sour milk, 1 cup butter, 1 teaspoon soda.

9. 1 lb. sugar, ½ lb. butter, 4 eggs, 1 cup sour milk, 1 teaspoon soda.

WHITE AND BLACK CAKES.

WHITE CAKES.

1. Whites of 9 eggs, 1 pt. icing sugar, 2 pts. sifted flour, 1 cup butter, ¾ cup milk, 3 teaspoons baking powder, whites of eggs beaten to a stiff froth, sugar and whites beaten together, butter worked to a cream, add the milk and a little flour, then put all together, beat well, flavor to taste, and bake 1 hour.

2. 2 cups sugar, ¾ cup butter, whites of 5 eggs, 1 cup sweet milk, 2 teaspoons baking powder.

3. 3 cups sugar, 1 cup butter, 1 cup milk, 4 cups flour, the whites of 8 eggs, 1 teaspoon soda, 2 teaspoons cream tartar.

4. Whites 12 eggs, 3 cups sugar, 1 cup butter, 1 cup sweet milk, 1 teaspoon soda, 2 teaspoons cream tartar, 5 cups flour, flavor if desired with bitter almonds.

5. ½ cup butter, 2 cups sugar, 1 cup milk, 3 cups flour, whites of 3 eggs, 1 teaspoon soda, 2 teaspoons cream tartar.

6. 3 cups sifted flour, 1½ cups sugar, 1 cup sweet milk, 1 egg, 2 tablespoons butter, 2 teaspoons cream tartar, 1 teaspoon soda, and a little essence of lemon.

BLACK CAKES.

7. 2 cups molasses, 1 cup sugar, 1 cup buttermilk, 1 cup shortening, 4 eggs, 1 teaspoon soda, 5½ cups flour, spice with cinnamon and cloves.

8. 1 lb. sugar, 1 lb. flour, 2½ lbs. raisins, 2½ lbs. currants, 1 lb. citron, mace, nutmegs, cinnamon, cloves, and bitter almonds, 1 wine glass brandy, 1 wine glass wine, 1 wine glass molasses, and 12 eggs.

LEMON CAKES.

1. 3 cups sugar, 1 cup butter, 5 eggs, 1 teaspoon soda, 1 teaspoon cream tartar, 1 cup sour milk, 4 cups flour, 1 grated lemon, sugar, butter, yolks to be beaten to a cream, the whites to a froth, and added last.

2. 1 lb. sugar, 6 eggs, ¼ lb. butter, 1 cup cream or thick milk, 4 cups flour, 1 teaspoon soda, 2 teaspoons cream tartar, the juice and rind of 1 lemon.

3. 1½ cups white sugar, ½ cup butter, ½ cup sweet milk, 2½ cups flour, 3 eggs, 1 teaspoon soda, 2 teaspoons cream tartar, 1 lemon.

4. 1 lb. sugar, 1 cup butter, 1 grated lemon, 1 cup sweet milk, 4 cups flour, 1 teaspoon soda, 1 teaspoon cream tartar, 5 eggs, beat the whites separately.

5. 1 lb. sugar, 5 cups flour, 1 cup sweet milk, 1 cup butter, 1 lemon, 5 eggs, 1 teaspoon cream tartar, 1 teaspoon soda.

ORANGE CAKES.

1. 2 cups sugar, 2 cups flour, the yolks of 5 eggs, the whites of 3, 1 orange, ½ cup of cold water, 3 teaspoons baking powder, grate the rind and squeeze the juice.

Dressing.—The whites of 2 eggs beaten to a stiff froth, rind and juice of an orange, make stiff with icing sugar, and spread as for jelly cake.

2. 12 eggs beaten separately, weight of 10 eggs in sugar, weight of 6 eggs in flour, juice and rind of 1 orange, making an icing of the whites of 2 eggs, 1 lb. icing sugar, 3 grated oranges, and add as a jelly.

3. 2 cups sugar, 1 cup butter, 3 cups flour, 6 eggs, 1 cup sweet milk, 1 small teaspoon soda, 2 teaspoons cream tartar.

Filling.—¼ lb. butter, ¼ lb. sugar, yolks of 3 eggs—2 large oranges mixed and let come to a boil, use whites of the eggs for icing top and sides of the cake.

Lemon can be used in the same manner.

MOLASSES CAKES OR GINGERBREAD.

1. 1 cup butter, 2 cups molasses, (or 1 cup molasses and 1 cup sugar,) 2 eggs, well beaten, 1 teaspoon saleratus, 1 cup milk, (sweet or sour,) but if sour then heap your spoon with saleratus, add flour to the consistency of pound cake.

2. 1 pt. New Orleans molasses, 3 eggs, 5 cups flour, 3 cups sugar, ½ pt. sour milk, 1 cup lard, 2 teaspoons soda, 3 teaspoons cream tartar, ginger. Put soda and cream tartar in milk, and put in last.

3. 2 cups molasses, 1 cup sugar, 1 cup water, ¾ cup shortening, 2 eggs, spice to taste, flour to make stiff enough, 1 tablespoon soda.

4. 2 cups molasses, 1 cup sugar, 1 cup water, ¾ cup shortening, 3 eggs, spice to taste, flour to make stiff enough, 1 tablespoon soda.

5. 1 pt. baking molasses, 1 cup brown sugar, 1 cup butter and lard mixed, 4 eggs, 1 teaspoon soda, 1 teaspoon cream tartar, 1 tablespoon cloves, 1 tablespoon cinnamon, 4 cups flour.

6. 1 cup molasses and 1 tablespoon soda beaten together until foamy, ½ cup water, butter the size of an egg, add flour enough to thicken sufficiently.

7. 1 qt. molasses, 1 cup sour milk, 2 cups shortening, 2 tablespoons ginger, 2 teaspoons soda, 6 eggs.

8. 4 cups molasses, 1 cup brown sugar, 2 cups butter, 2 cups sour cream, 2 tablespoons soda, 2 tablespoons ginger, 6 eggs.

9. 2 cups molasses, ½ cup sugar, 1 cup cream or sour milk, 1 cup melted butter, 3 eggs, 1 tablespoon ginger, 1 tablespoon cinnamon, 1 tablespoon soda, ½ nutmeg, 5 cups flour, and bake in pans.

10. 4 cups flour, 1 cup butter, 2 cups molasses, 1 cup brown sugar, 4 eggs, 1 teaspoon soda, 1 tablespoon ginger.

11. 1 pt. molasses, ½ pt. buttermilk, ¼ pt. lard, 1 tablespoon ginger, 1 tablespoon soda, scalded in the buttermilk.

12. 1 qt. molasses, 1 pt. buttermilk, ½ pt. butter, 1 tablespoon ginger, 1 tablespoon, heaping full, soda.

13. 1 qt. molasses, 1 pt. buttermilk, ½ tin cup lard, 1 tablespoon soda, 2 teaspoons ginger. Stir very soft.

14. 1 pt. molasses, 1 cup lard, 1 tablespoon ginger, 1 pt. sour milk, 1 egg, 1 tablespoon soda, 3 pts. sifted flour, spread in pans about half an inch thick.

15. 1 pt. molasses, $\frac{1}{2}$ pt. sour milk, $\frac{1}{2}$ lb. lard, 1 cup sugar, 1 tablespoon soda, 1 nutmeg.

16. 1 cup molasses, 1 cup butter, 1 cup sugar, 1 cup milk, 3 cups flour, 3 eggs, 1 teaspoon soda. Spice to taste.

17. 1 cup molasses, 1 cup sugar, $\frac{1}{2}$ cup butter, 1 large teaspoon soda, mix the sugar, molasses and soda thoroughly, take half cup butter, and fill the remainder up with boiling water, and add the last thing before the flour. Flour to roll soft, with ginger to taste.

18. 1 cup butter, 1 cup sugar, 3 eggs, 1 cup molasses, 1 teaspoon ginger, $\frac{1}{2}$ teaspoon cloves, $\frac{1}{2}$ teaspoon soda, 3 cups flour.

19. $\frac{3}{4}$ pound flour, 1 qt. molasses, $\frac{1}{4}$ pound butter, 1 oz. saleratus, 1 oz. ginger.

20. 1 qt. molasses, 2 tablespoons ginger, 4 eggs, 1 pt. warm water, $\frac{1}{2}$ pt. lard, $2\frac{1}{2}$ pts. flour, 1 oz. soda.

21. 1 qt. molasses, 1 qt. buttermilk, $1\frac{1}{2}$ cups lard, 1 cup vinegar, 1 tablespoon ginger, 2 tablespoons soda dissolved in the vinegar, $1\frac{1}{2}$ cups sugar.

22. 2 cups molasses, 1 cup lard, 1 teaspoon ginger, 1 teaspoon cream tartar, dissolve in water, enough flour to make smooth.

23. 1 pt. molasses, 1 cup shortening, 1 cup sour milk, 2 eggs, spice to taste, two teaspoons soda, 1 teaspoon cream tartar.

24. 1 qt. molasses, $1\frac{1}{2}$ tins buttermilk, 3 tablespoons even full soda, $\frac{3}{4}$ of a tin of lard.

25. 2 cups molasses, 1 cup sugar, 5 cups flour, 1 cup shortening, 2 eggs, 1 tablespoon soda, 1 do. ginger, soda mixed with flour.

26. 1 cup molasses, 1 cup warm water, 1 teaspoon ginger, 1 teaspoon soda, 4 tablespoons melted butter, stir flour in very thin.

TWO OR MORE ALIKE.

FRENCH CAKES.

1. 3 cups white sugar, $\frac{3}{4}$ cup butter, 1 cup sweet milk, 4 cups flour, 3 teaspoons baking powder, 3 eggs, little salt, 1 lemon skin grated, and beat butter and sugar to a cream.

2. 2 cups sugar, $\frac{1}{2}$ cup butter, 3 cups flour, 3 eggs, 2 teaspoons cream tartar, 1 teaspoon soda, 1 cup milk.

3. 3 cups bread sponge, 2 cups white sugar, 1 cup butter, 3 eggs, 1 nutmeg, 1 small teaspoon saleratus, put the butter, sugar and eggs together, 1 lb. seeded raisins.

4. 1 lb. flour, ¾ lb. sugar, ½ lb. butter, 1 lb. raisins, ½ cup sour cream, 8 eggs, 1 teaspoon soda, nutmeg.

SNOW CAKES.

1. 1 cup butter, 3 cups sugar, 3½ cups flour, ½ cup sweet milk, whites of 10 eggs, 1½ teaspoons baking powder, stir in the flour quickly, and bake in 3 tins.

2. Whites of 10 eggs, 1½ tumblers sugar, 1 tumbler flour, 1 teaspoon cream tartar.

3. 2 cups sugar, 1 cup butter, 3 cups flour, 1 cup milk, whites of 8 eggs, use part corn starch, 1 teaspoon soda, 3 teaspoons cream tartar, and flavor to taste.

4. ½ cup butter, 1 cup milk, 2 cups sugar, 2½ cups flour, whites of 4 eggs, 2 teaspoons yeast powder.

5. 3 eggs, 1½ cups sugar, ½ cup butter, ½ cup milk, 2 cups flour, 2 teaspoons of baking powder, ice them between and sprinkle cocoanut.

SWEET WILLIAM CAKES.

1. 3 cups sugar, 3 eggs, 3 cups buttermilk or sour milk, 1 cup butter or lard, 1 nutmeg, 1 teaspoon soda, and bake in lard.

2. 3 cups sugar, 3 eggs, 1½ cups milk, 1 cup butter, 1 nutmeg, 1 teaspoon of soda, and bake in lard.

SPICE CAKES.

1. 1 cup butter, 3 cups brown sugar, 1 cup molasses, yolks of 10 eggs, 1 cup sour cream, 1 teaspoon soda, 1 teaspoon cinnamon, cloves, allspice and nutmeg, and 4 cups flour.

2. 1 cup butter, 2 cups sugar, ½ cup buttermilk, ½ cup molasses, 3 cups flour, 1 cup raisins, 3 eggs, 1 teaspoon soda, 1 tablespoon cloves, 1 tablespoon cinnamon.

3. 1 cup butter, 2 eggs, 1½ cups sugar beat well together, 1 cup sour milk, 4 cups flour, ¼ teaspoon cloves, ¼ teaspoon allspice, 1 teaspoon cinnamon, ½ nutmeg, and grated rind of lemon.

4. 1 cups brown sugar, 3 cups flour, 1 cup sour cream, ½ cup butter, 5 eggs, whites of 3 left out, 1 nutmeg, 1 teaspoon cinnamon, 1 teaspoon cloves, 1 teaspoon cream tartar, 1 teaspoon soda. Icing in layers, made of the three whites with 2 cups icing sugar, or as jelly cake.

5. 2 cups brown sugar, 3 cups flour, 1 cup sour cream, ½ cup butter, 5 eggs, the whites of 4 left out, 1 nutmeg, 1 teaspoon cinnamon, 1 teaspoon cloves, 1 teaspoon soda, 1 teaspoon cream tartar. Bake in layers as for jelly cake, take the whites of the four eggs with one cup white sugar for icing.

TIP-TOP CAKES.

1. 1½ cups sugar, 1 cup sweet milk, 2 eggs, 2½ cups flour, 2 teaspoons cream tartar in the flour, butter the size of an egg, 1 teaspoon soda in the milk.

2. 3 cups sugar, 2 cups sweet milk, 2 tablespoons butter, 3 eggs, 2 teaspoons cream tartar, 1½ teaspoons soda, 4½ cups flour.

SPANISH CAKES.

1. 1 lb. sugar, ¼ lb. butter, 1 oz. soda, ½ oz. alum, 1 tin cup thick milk, make a soft dough, roll and cut in squares.

2. 2 lbs. sugar, ½ lb. butter, 2 oz. soda, 1 oz. alum, 1 qt. sour milk.

3. 3 lbs. sugar, ¾ lb. butter, 1 tablespoon soda in 1 qt. milk; beat butter soft, add sugar, mix well, then add milk and flour. Make very soft; oven not too warm.

TEA CAKES.

1. 4 eggs, 1 cup butter, 1 cup sour milk, 3 cups flour, 2 cups white sugar, 1 teaspoon soda, bake in a square pan.

2. 1½ cups sugar, 1 egg, 1 tablespoon butter, 1 teaspoon soda, 2 teaspoons cream tartar, 1 cup sour milk.

3. 4 eggs, 1 cup sugar, 1 teaspoon baking powder, 1 cup flour, 1 teaspoon extract lemon, bake in long pans.

4. 1 cup sugar, 1 cup butter, 1 cup milk, 2 eggs, 1 teaspoon soda.

5. 4 cups flour, 3 of sugar, 1 cup butter, 3 eggs, 1 cup milk, 1 spoonful saleratus.

6. 2 teacups sweet milk, 1 teaspoon soda, 2½ cups corn meal, 1 cup molasses, 2 eggs, 2 cups flour, 1 teaspoon ginger, bake half an hour.

DOVER CAKES.

1. 2 cups of sugar, 1 cup butter, 1 cup sweet milk, 4 cups flour, 5 eggs, 2 teaspoons cream tartar, 1 teaspoon soda.

2. 1 lb. white sugar, ½ lb. creamed butter, 2 tin cups sifted flour, ½ tin cup sour milk, 1 teaspoon soda, 2 teaspoons cream tartar, dissolved in vinegar, 1 lemon.

3. 1 lb. sugar, 3¼ lbs. flour, 5 eggs, ½ lb. butter.

4. 1 lb. white sugar, ½ lb. butter, 5 eggs, 1 teaspoon soda, 2 teaspoons cream tartar, 1 pt. sour milk, 2 tin cups flour.

5. 1 lb. brown sugar, ½ lb. butter, 1 lb. flour, 1 cup sour milk, 6 eggs beaten separately, ½ lb. raisins, some citron, 1 tablespoon cinnamon, 1 teaspoon cloves, 1 nutmeg, beat butter and sugar to a cream; then put in the yolks and spices, then the milk and flour; save a little of the flour to rub in the raisins; one teaspoon soda dissolved in a little hot water; the raisins in last, or just before the whites. Bake one hour and a half.

CLAY CAKES.

1. 1 lb. sugar, 6 eggs, 1 cup butter, 1 cup sweet milk, 5 cups flour, 2 teaspoons baking powder. Flavor to taste.

2. 1 lb. sugar, 6 eggs, 2 cups sour cream, $\frac{1}{2}$ cup butter, 4 cups flour, 1 teaspoon soda, 1 teaspoon cream tartar. Spice with lemon.

BUCKEYE CAKES.

1. 3 cups sugar, 6 eggs, 1 cup sour milk, 1 cup butter, 4 cups flour, 1 teaspoon cream tartar, 1 teaspoon soda. Bake in square pans.

2. 1 lb. sugar, 6 eggs, 1 cup butter, 1 cup sour milk, 1 teaspoon soda, 2 teaspoons cream tartar, 2 lbs. flour.

STRAW CAKES.

1. 1 lb. sugar, 6 eggs, 1 cup butter, 1 cup sour cream, $\frac{1}{2}$ teaspoon soda, 1 teaspoon cream tartar, 4 cups flour. Flavor.

2. 5 eggs, 3 cups sugar, 1 cup butter, 1 cup sweet cream, 4 cups flour, 1 teaspoon soda, 2 teaspoons cream tartar. Flavor with lemon.

ICE-CREAM CAKES.

1. 2 cups sugar, 1 cup butter, 1 cup milk, 1 cup corn starch, 2 cups flour, whites of 8 eggs, 1 teaspoon soda, 2 teaspoons cream tartar. Flavor with vanilla.

2. 1 cup sugar, 2 cups flour, $\frac{1}{2}$ cup sour milk, 3 eggs, $\frac{1}{2}$ cup butter, 1 teaspoon cream tartar, $\frac{1}{2}$ teaspoon soda. Flavor with vanilla.

SODA CAKE.

1. $2\frac{1}{2}$ cups sugar, 4 eggs, 1 cup butter, 1 cup cream, 4 cups flour, 1 teaspoon soda, 1 teaspoon cream tartar.

2. 2 cups sugar, 2 cups sour cream, 2 tin cups flour, 3 eggs, 2 teaspoons soda, 3 teaspoons cream tartar.

3. 3 cups sugar, $1\frac{1}{2}$ cups butter, 5 eggs, 1 cup water, 1 teaspoon soda dissolved in it, 2 teaspoons cream tartar, 5 cups flour, 1 nutmeg. Bake like jelly cake.

BRIDE CAKE.

1. Whites of 10 eggs, 2 cups pulverized sugar, 1 cup flour, 1 teaspoon cream tartar. Put all into a sieve, and sift all on the whites.

2. Whites of 10 eggs, well beaten, 2 cups pulverized sugar, 1 cup flour, 1 teaspoon cream tartar. Put all except the eggs into a sieve, and sift on the eggs.

BOSTON CAKE.

1. 1 lb. sugar, 1 do. flour, $\frac{1}{2}$ do. butter, 8 eggs, 2 teaspoons cream tartar, 1 do. soda, 1 glass milk. Rub the cream tartar in the flour, mix yolks of eggs, sugar and butter together.

2. 2 cups sugar, 3 eggs, 1 cup sour milk, 3 cups flour, 1 tablespoon butter, 1 teaspoon soda, essence of lemon.

PEARL CAKE.

1. 1 tincup flour, 1 do. sugar, 1 teacup cornstarch, 1 teacup sweet milk, 1 do. butter, 1 teaspoon baking powder, and the whites of 6 eggs beaten to a stiff froth.

2. 1 cup butter, 2 do. sugar, 1 do. sweet milk, 2 do. flour, 1 do. cornstarch, whites of 8 eggs, 2 teaspoons baking powder.

3. 1 cup butter, 2 do. sugar, 1 do. milk, 1½ do. cornstarch, 2½ do. flour, whites of 5 eggs, 1 teaspoon soda, 2 teaspoons cream tartar.

SURPRISE CAKE.

1. ¾ cup butter, 1 do. sweet milk, 2 do. sugar, 1 egg, 1 teaspoon soda, 2 teaspoons cream tartar, 2 cups flour, flavor to taste.

2. 1 egg, 1 cup sugar, ½ do. butter, 1 do. sweet milk, 1 teaspoon soda, 2 teaspoons cream tartar, flavor with lemon; flour sufficient.

3. 1 egg, 1 cup sugar, ½ do. butter, 1 do. sweet milk, 1 teaspoon soda, 2 teaspoons cream tartar, flavor with lemon. Sufficient flour to make good batter.

COTTAGE CAKE.

1. 3 cups sugar, 1 do. butter, 2 eggs, 2 cups sweet milk, 2 teaspoons soda, 4 do. cream tartar, 1 lb. raisins, ½ do. citron, 1 quart flour.

2. 1 cup lard, 2 do. sugar, 2 do. sweet milk, 2 eggs, 2 teaspoons cream tartar, 1 do. soda, 4 cups flour. By putting raisins in, you will have a fruit cake.

3. 1 cup butter, 3 do. sugar, 2 do. sweet milk, 1 quart flour mixed with 4 teaspoons cream tartar, 2 teaspoons soda dissolved in the milk, 2 eggs, 1 lb. raisins, ½ do. citron. Make a large cake, put the ingredients in as written down.

RAILROAD CAKE.

1. 4 eggs, 3 cups flour, 3 do. sugar, 1 tablespoon sweet milk, 1 teaspoon soda, 2 do. cream tartar.

2. 1 cup sugar, 1 do. flour, 3 tablespoons sweet milk, 3 eggs, 1 teaspoon cream tartar, ½ do. soda, butter the size of an egg, bake in a square pan.

MISCELLANEOUS CAKES.

WATERMELON CAKE.—*White Part.*—2 cups white sugar, 1 cup butter, 3 cups flour, ½ cup sweet milk, 1 teaspoon cream tartar, ½ teaspoon soda, whites of 8 eggs. Flavor with lemon.

Red Part.—1 cup red sugar, ½ cup butter, 1½ cups flour, whites of 4 eggs, ¼ cup sweet milk, ½ teaspoon cream tartar, ¼ teaspoon soda, 1 cup seeded raisins, floured and mixed in the dough. Put half the white dough in the pan first, then all the red and the other half of the white.

Clove Cake.—1 cup butter, 2 cups sugar, 1 cup buttermilk, 1 teaspoon soda, 1 egg, nearly 1 teaspoon each of cinnamon and cloves. Raisins or currants improve it.

Irish Rag Cake.—3 cups sugar, 1 cup butter, 1 cup sour cream, 6 eggs, 8 cups flour, 1 teaspoon soda, 2 teaspoons cream tartar.

Lady Cake.—3 cups butter, 2 cups sugar, 1 cup sour cream or milk, 3 cups flour, 2 teaspoons cream tartar, 1 teaspoon soda, whites of 8 eggs. Flavor with bitter almonds.

Number Cake.—1 cup butter, 1 cup cream, 2 cups sugar, 3 cups flour, 4 eggs, 1 teaspoon cream tartar, ½ teaspoon soda.

Harrison Cake.—2 well-beaten eggs, ½ lb. sugar, 1 tablespoon butter, ½ teacup sweet milk, ½ teaspoon saleratus, ¼ a nutmeg, flour enough to make a smooth batter.

Union Cake.—2½ cups flour, 1½ cups sugar, ½ cup lard, ½ cup milk, 3 eggs beaten well, 1 teaspoon soda, 2 teaspoons cream tartar. Bake half an hour.

Rice Cake.—Beat yolks of 15 eggs nearly half an hour, mix well with them 10 oz. fine sifted loaf sugar, put in ½ lb. ground rice, a little orange water or brandy, the grated rinds of 2 lemons, then add the whites of 7 eggs, well beaten, stir all together for a quarter of an hour. Put into a hoop and set in a quick oven for half an hour, when it will be done.

Citron Cake.—2 cups sugar, 4 cups flour, ¾ cup butter, 1 cup sweet milk, whites of 8 eggs, 1 cup chopped citron, 3 teaspoons baking powder.

Bread Cake.—3 cups light dough, 3 eggs, 2 cups sugar, 1 teaspoon cinnamon, 1 teaspoon cloves, 1½ cups butter, ½ teaspoon soda, 1 cup raisins.

Pork Cake.—2 cups raw fat pork out of salt brine, chop fine, pour over it 2 cups boiling water, after it cools 2 cups molasses, 2 cups brown sugar, 1 cup currants, 1 teaspoon soda, 2 teaspoons cream tartar. Bake in pans.

Lizzie's Cake.—1 cup butter, 3 cups sugar, 1 cup milk, 4 cups flour, 4 eggs, whites and yolks beaten separately, 2 teaspoons cream tartar, 1 teaspoon soda. Dark spices.

Governor's Cake.—1 lb. butter, 1 lb. powdered loaf sugar, 1 grated nutmeg, 1 tablespoon cinnamon, 4 large tablespoons caraway seeds, 1 wineglass rosewater. Mix the whole with sufficient cold water to make a stiff dough.

Home Cake.—1 cup butter, 2 cups sugar, 4 cups flour, 1 cup milk, 5 eggs, 2 teaspoons cream tartar, 1 teaspoon soda. Flavor with nutmeg.

Guess Cake.—1 cup butter, 2 cups sugar, 3 cups flour, 4 eggs, 1 cup buttermilk.

Puff Cake.—2 cups sugar, ½ cup butter, 1 cup sweet milk, 3 cups flour, 3 eggs, ½ teaspoon soda, 1 teaspoon cream tartar, 2 teaspoons vanilla. Bake with a quick heat.

Elegant Cake.—Dissolve 1 teaspoon soda in one cup sweet milk, 1 tablespoon cream tartar, 1½ cups sugar, 2 eggs, 2½ cups sifted flour, 1 tablespoon butter, spice to taste. Bake in a quick oven.

Poor Man's Cake.—1 cup sugar, 1 cup sour milk, ¾ cup butter, 1 teaspoon soda, 2½ cups flour. Beat all together and bake like pound cake.

Aunt Jemima's Cake.—4 cups sugar, 4 eggs, 1 cup butter, 2 teaspoons soda, 4 teaspoons cream tartar.

Social Cake.—1 cup butter, 2 do. sugar, 3½ do. flour, 4 eggs, beaten separately, ¾ cup milk, 1 teaspoon cream tartar, ½ do. soda. Flavor with lemon.

Black Dough.—1 cup melted butter, 2 do. brown sugar, 1 do. molasses, 1 do. sour cream, 1 teaspoon soda, 4 cups flour, yolks of 8 eggs, 1 nutmeg, 1 tablespoon cinnamon, 1 do. allspice.

Anonymous Cake.—1 tin cup flour, ½ cup butter or lard, 2 eggs, 1 cup sugar, 1 do. sour milk, 1 teaspoon cream tartar, 1 do. soda, 1 do. salt. Bake 20 minutes.

Lafayette Cake.—2 cups white sugar, 3 eggs, 1 cup sour milk, 1 do. butter, 3 do. flour, 1 teaspoon cream tartar in the flour, 1 do. soda in the milk.

Harvest Cake.—2 cups sugar, 1 do. sour cream, 2 eggs, 2 teaspoons cream tartar, 1 do. soda.

Miss Barton's Cake.—½ lb. butter, 1 lb. sugar, 6 eggs, 1 lb. flour, 1 cup sour cream, ½ nutmeg, 1 teaspoon soda.

Bernard Cakes.—2 cups sugar, 1 do. sour milk, 3 eggs, 1 small cup butter, 3¾ cups flour, 1 teaspoon soda.

Yellow Cake.—2 cups sugar, 1 do. butter, 1 do. milk, 4 do. flour, the yolks of 8 eggs, 1 teaspoon soda, 2 do. cream tartar.

Rough Cake.—3 cups sugar, 1 do. butter, 1 do. thick cream, 5 do. flour, 6 eggs, 1 teaspoon soda.

Log Cabin Cake.—1 lb. sugar, 1 cup sour cream, 6 eggs, 1 teaspoon soda.

Best Cake in the World.—1 lb. white sugar, 6 eggs, 1 cup butter, 1 do. sour cream, 1 teaspoon soda, 2 do. cream tartar, 4 cups flour, beat the yolks, butter and cream together, then add whites and flour, then the soda.

Centre Cake.—6 eggs, 2 cups sugar, 2 do. flour, 4 tablespoons sweet cream, 1 teaspoon soda, 2 do. cream tartar, beat the yolks of eggs and sugar together. Whites should be beaten separately.

Jenny Lind Cake.—6 eggs, 2 cups sugar, 4 do. flour, 1 do. butter, 1 do. cream, 1 teaspoon soda, 1 do. cream tartar.

Matrimonial Cake.—3 eggs, 1½ cups cream, 2 do. sugar, ½ teaspoon soda, flour to make a thin batter, spread as thin as possible on square tins and bake; take off from the tins while hot, and place a thin layer of currant jelly between slices of the cake.

Huckleberry Cake.—4 eggs, 3 cups sugar, 1 do. butter, 2 do. milk, 3 do. berries, 6 do. flour, 1 teaspoon soda.

Rich Seed Cake.—1¼ lbs. flour, 1 lb. butter, 1 lb. loaf sugar, beat and stiffen, 8 eggs, 2 oz. caraway seed, one grated nutmeg and its weight in cinnamon, beat the whites of the eggs to a froth and the yolks separately, then mix them with the butter and sugar, beat in the flour, spices and seed. Bake two hours.

Honey Cake.—2 cups sugar, 1 cup sour cream, 2 eggs, 1 teaspoon soda, 1 teaspoon cream tartar. Flour to stiffen.

Neapolitan Cake.—*Black Part.*—1 cup butter, 2 do. brown sugar, 1 do. molasses, 1 do. of strong coffee, 4½ do. sifted flour, 4 eggs, 2 teaspoons soda, 2 teaspoons cinnamon, 2 teaspoons cloves, 1 teaspoon mace, 1½ lbs. raisins, 1½ lbs. currants, ¾ lb. citron. Bake in round straight-sided pans, 1¼ inches thick when baked.

White Part.—1 cup butter, 4 cups powdered white sugar, 2 do. sweet milk, 2 do. cornstarch mixed with flour, whites of 8 eggs, 6 teaspoons baking powder, flavor slightly with bitter almonds. Bake in same pans and as nearly as possible same thickness as black part. When the cakes are cold, spread with the following: White of 1 egg thoroughly beaten, grated rind of 2 lemons, juice of 3, powdered sugar enough to make thick frosting. Use no flavoring. Then lay in alternate layers of black and white, with icing between each layer.

A Good Cake.—1 lb. sugar, 6 eggs, 1 cup butter, 4 cups flour, 2 teaspoons cream tartar, 1 teaspoon soda, mix butter, sugar and yolks to a cream, beat whites to a froth, then add whites, flour and soda.

Loaf Cake.—4 eggs, 4 cups flour, 1½ do. butter, 1½ do. sugar, 1 cup yeast, 1 teaspoon soda, 1 cup cream.

Temperance Cake.—1 lb. sugar, 6 eggs, ¾ lb. butter, 1 nutmeg, 2 lbs. flour, 1 teaspoon soda. Roll thin, sprinkle sugar over and bake quick.

Walnut Cake.—1 lb. sugar, 1 qt. walnut kernels, the whites of 6 eggs, 8 tablespoons flour. Drop on tins.

Almond Cake.—2 cups of sugar, 2 do. milk, 1 teaspoon melted butter, 1 teaspoon soda, 2 eggs, nutmeg. Bake in fat.

Wedding Cake.—4 lbs. flour, 3 lbs. butter, 3 lbs. sugar, 4 lbs. currants, 2 lbs. raisins, 2 doz. eggs, 1 oz. mace, and 3 nutmegs; a little citron and molasses improves it. Bake about three hours.

Measure Cake.—1 cup butter, 2 cups sugar, 3 eggs, ½ teaspoon soda dissolved in one cup milk, 1 teaspoon cream tartar, 5 cups flour. Stir the butter and sugar to a cream, add the eggs, the whites and yolks beaten separately, then the soda and milk, and lastly the cream tartar and flour; flavor as you please. Bake in small tins or in a loaf.

Queen Cake.—10 eggs, 3 qts. flour, 1 lb. sugar, nutmeg. Beat till light and bake in pans.

Apies.—2 cups sugar, 1 cup butter, 4 eggs, ½ cup flour, 1 teaspoon yeast powder.

Composition Cake.—1 lb. flour, 1 cup of sugar, ½ lb. butter, 7 eggs, ½ pt. cream.

Union Cake.—1 cup butter, 2 cups sugar, 1 cup sweet milk, 3 cups flour, ½ cup cornstarch, 4 eggs, ½ teaspoon soda, 1 teaspoon cream tartar, and essence.

Cousin's Cake.—1½ cups sugar, 2 tablespoons butter, 1 egg, 2 cups flour, 1 cup sweet milk, 1 teaspoon soda, 2 teaspoons cream tartar.

Farmer's Cake.—2 cups sugar, 1 cup sweet milk, ¾ cup butter, 3 eggs, 3 cups flour, 1 teaspoon soda, 2 teaspoons cream tartar, essence.

Editor's Cake.—1 cup sugar, 1 egg, beat egg and sugar till light, then add 1 cup sour cream, 1 teaspoon soda, nutmeg and cinnamon to taste, and 3 cups flour.

Metropolitan Cake.—2 cups white sugar, ½ cup butter, 1 cup sweet milk, 1 cup corn starch, 2 cups flour, whites of 4 eggs, 3 teaspoons baking powder. This is the white part.
Dark Part.—1 cup brown sugar, ½ cup butter, ½ cup molasses, ½ cup of strong coffee, 2¼ cups flour, 1 teaspoon baking powder, 1 teaspoon cinnamon, 1 teaspoon cloves, and 1 nutmeg. Bake in jelly rings.

Coffee Cake.—1 cup brown sugar, 1 cup butter, 1 cup strained coffee, 1 cup molasses, 3 eggs well beaten, 1 lb. raisins, 2 cups flour, 2 teaspoons baking powder.

Lady Cake.—½ lb. butter, ¾ lb. sugar, whites of 16 eggs, 40 drops essence bitter almonds, ½ gill rosewater, 3 lbs. flour. Mix as pound cake.

Washington Cake.—1 lb. sugar, 1 cup butter, 3 eggs, ½ a tin of thick milk, 1 teaspoon soda, 1 teaspoon cream tartar, 4½ cups flour. Beat the butter, eggs and sugar to a cream, then add the rest.

Yeast Cake.—Take 2½ lbs. flour, 2 lbs. currants, 2 lbs. butter, ½ lb. moist sugar, ½ ounce pounded spice, 4 yolks and 2 whites of eggs, a tablespoon of yeast, and a little warm water. Mix all together and put it before the fire to rise for about an hour, then make into cakes.

Cheap Cake.—1 cup sugar, 1 egg, ½ cup buttermilk, 1 tablespoon butter, ½ teaspoon soda, flour enough to make a stiff batter. Flavor with lemon.

LIGHT CAKE.—Take 4 cups flour, 3 cups sugar, 1 cup butter, 1 cup sweet milk, 4 eggs, 1 teaspoon soda, 1 teaspoon cream tartar. Flavor to taste.

CIDER CAKE.—6 cups flour, 3 cups sugar, 1 cup butter, 4 eggs, 1 cup cider, 1 teaspoon soda, 1 nutmeg.

JENNY LIND CAKE.—2 cups sugar, 3 cups flour, 1 cup milk, ½ cup butter, 2 eggs, 1 teaspoon soda, 2 teaspoons cream tartar. Flavor with nutmeg.

FOURTH CAKE.—3 eggs, 2 cups sugar, 1 cup thick milk, 1 cup butter, 1 teaspoon soda, 1 do. cream tartar, 3 cups flour.

INVALIDS' CAKE.—1 egg, fill up the cup with sweet cream, 1½ cups flour, 1 do. sugar, 1 teaspoon soda, 1½ do. cream tartar.

TAYLOR CAKE.—¾ lb. butter, ¾ do. sugar, 1 pt. sour milk, 1 quart molasses, 8 eggs, 1 tablespoon cinnamon, 1 do. ginger, 3 lbs. flour, 4 large tablespoons soda.

ROCHESTER CAKE.—1¾ lbs. sugar, 8 eggs, ½ lb. butter, 1 pt. sour cream or buttermilk. Flour to make as stiff as pound cake, 1 teaspoon soda, 1 do. cream tartar. Flavor with lemon or vanilla.

BREAKFAST CAKE.—2 cups sweet milk, ½ do. sugar, 4 do. flour, 2 eggs, 2 teaspoons soda, 4 do. cream tartar. Bake in a quick oven.

ICINGS.

1. 2 cups sugar, 1 cup water, boil to a thick syrup, beat the whites of 4 eggs to a stiff froth, add the syrup while boiling to the eggs, beating the eggs briskly all the time.

2. Whites of 3 eggs, 1 lb. sugar, spread icing and grated cocoanut between layers, and over top and sides.

3. Whites of 2 eggs, to ½ lb. sugar, and beat it up until stiff.

4. *Chocolate Icing.*—Not quite a cup of milk, 1½ cups sugar, 2 oz. grated chocolate, boil together until quite stiff. Flavor with vanilla.

5. *Icing for Cocoanut Cake.*—1 pt. sweet cream, and the whites of 3 eggs beaten together, add 1 grated cocoanut, 6 tablespoons sugar, and 1 teaspoon vanilla.

6. *Chocolate Icing.*—1 cup sugar, ½ cup chocolate, ½ cup cream, a lump of butter, boil until a little stiff.

CHOCOLATE CARAMELS.

1. 1 cup sweet milk, 1 cup molasses, 1½ cups brown sugar, boil together 15 minutes, then add butter the size of a large walnut, rolled in a tablespoon flour. In the meantime melt ½ cake of baker's chocolate, add to it the other ingredients, boil until thick, then add 1 large tablespoon vanilla, try it as molasses candy, and when boiled enough, butter some pans, and pour in when nearly cold and cut in small squares.

2. ½ cup sweet milk, 6 tablespoons good molasses, ½ lb. sugar, 1 tablespoon butter, 1 square cake chocolate, boil well, pour in pans, and cut in small squares.

3. 1 cup molasses, 2 cups brown sugar, ½ cake grated chocolate, ½ cup sweet cream. Flavor if you wish; most prefer without. Put in the chocolate after it boils.

SMALL CAKES.

COOKIES.

1. 1 cup sugar, 1 cup butter, 1 cup cream, 1 teaspoon soda, 2 teaspoons cream tartar, 2 eggs, and flour to stiffen enough to roll.

2. 2 cups sugar, 1 cup butter, 3 eggs, 5 cups flour, 1 small teaspoon saleratus, 2 tablespoons sour cream, a little lemon.

3. 1 cup butter, 1 cup sweet milk, 2 cups sugar, 1 teaspoon soda, 2 teaspoons cream tartar; roll thin, cut in small cakes and bake in a quick oven.

4. 2 lbs. sugar, 1 lb. butter, 1 pt. sweet milk, 2 teaspoons soda. Flour enough to roll.

5. 1 cup sugar, 1 do. butter, ½ do. sour milk, ½ teaspoon soda.

6. 2 cups sugar, 1 do. butter, 2 eggs, 1 cup sour cream, 3 do. flour. Spices to taste.

7. 4 eggs, 3 cups sugar, 1 cup butter, 1 nutmeg, 1 teaspoon soda, 2 teaspoons cream tartar. Flour to roll.

8. 3 cups sugar, 1 do. butter, 2 eggs, 1½ cups cream, 1 teaspoon soda.

9. 1 cup lard, 1 do. sweet milk, 2 cups sugar, 2 well-beaten eggs, 1 teaspoon soda, nutmeg.

10. 1 cup butter, 3 do. sugar, 1 do. cold water, 1 teaspoon soda, 1 do. ginger. Roll thin and cut with tin.

11. 2 cups sugar, 1 do. butter, ½ do. sour milk, ½ teaspoon soda.

12. 1 cup butter, 2 do. sugar, 4 eggs, ½ cup sour cream, 1 teaspoon soda, 2 do. cream tartar; spice to taste, with enough flour to roll thin.

13. 2 cups brown sugar, 1 cup butter, 3 eggs, 1 tablespoon ginger, 1 teaspoon soda, work in flour to make a soft dough. Roll and cut into cakes.

14. 4 eggs, 1 qt. flour, 2 cups sugar, ¾ do. butter, 3 teaspoons yeast powder. Roll out and bake in a quick oven.

15. Take 2 cups molasses, 1 do. butter, 1 do. real full of shortening, 1 do. boiling water, 1 tablespoon soda, 1 do. ginger, 1 do. cinnamon; put all together and warm. Mix flour to roll out as other cookies.

16. 1 cup sugar, ⅔ do. butter, ½ do. sweet milk, 1 egg, 1 teaspoon saleratus, nutmeg.

JUMBLES.

1. 1 lb. sugar, ½ do. butter, 1 do. flour, 6 eggs, 1 teaspoon soda. Spice to taste.

2. 1 lb. flour, ¾ do. sugar, ½ do. butter, 5 eggs. Rosewater to taste.

3. 2 cups sugar, 1 do. butter, 2 teaspoons cream tartar, 1 do. soda, ½ cup cream, 5 eggs.

4. 1 lb. sugar, ¾ do. butter, 7 eggs, 1 cup milk, 1 teaspoon soda, flour to drop on pans.

5. 3 cups sugar, 1 do. butter, 6 eggs, ½ teaspoon soda, 1 do. cream tartar, flour to make soft dough. Flavor to taste, and bake a very light brown.

6. 1 cup butter, 1½ do. sugar, 1 egg, 1 do. sour cream, 1 teaspoon soda. When baked, cut them out and sprinkle cinnamon and sugar over them.

7. 1 cup butter, 2 do. sugar, 4 eggs, 1 teaspoon soda, 2 do. cream tartar, ½ cup sour cream, nutmeg.

8. 1 lb. white sugar, ¾ do. butter, 1¼ do. flour, 5 eggs. Flavor with mace and lemon.

9. 1 egg, 1 cup sugar, ½ do. butter, 2 tablespoons buttermilk, 1 teaspoon cream tartar, ½ do. soda. Flavor with lemon, mix rather stiff, roll, and cut with cutter.

10. 1½ cups sugar, ½ cup butter, 3 eggs, ½ cup cream, 1 tablespoon cream tartar, ½ tablespoon soda, flour to make a stiff dough.

11. 4 eggs, 3 cups sugar, 1 nutmeg, 1 cup butter, 4 do. flour, 1 teaspoon soda. Roll them and sprinkle with sugar.

12. 2 cups sugar, 1 cup bread sponge, 1 do. sour cream, 1 teaspoon soda, 2 eggs.

TAYLOR CAKES.

1. 1 pt. molasses, 3 eggs, ¾ pt. melted butter and lard, 1 cup sugar, 1 do. sour milk, 1 tablespoon soda, 1 do. cinnamon, ½ do. ginger, 1½ do. cloves, make a little stiffer than pound cake, drop in pans and bake in a quick oven.

2. 1 pt. molasses, ½ lb. butter, ½ do. brown sugar, 4 eggs, ½ pt. sour milk, 1 tablespoon soda, ginger, cloves, and cinnamon to taste. Drop on tins.

3. 1 lb. butter, ¾ lb. sugar, 8 eggs, 1 pt. thick milk, 1 qt. molasses, 3 lbs. flour, 2 oz. soda. Spice to taste.

4. 1 cup butter, 1 do. sour cream, 1 do. sugar, 5 eggs, 1 pt. molasses, 1 tablespoon saleratus, 1 do. ginger, 1 do. cinnamon.

5. 1 qt. molasses, ½ lb. sugar, 4 eggs, 1 pt. thick or buttermilk, 6 oz. melted lard, 1 large teaspoon soda, 2 lbs. flour. Spice to taste, and drop on pans, with ginger or cloves.

GINGER CAKES.

1. 1 pt. molasses, 1 oz. ginger, ½ oz. cloves, 1½ lbs. flour.

2. 2 cups molasses, 2 do. sugar, 4 eggs, 1 cup butter, 1 do. milk or cream, 1½ teaspoons soda, 6 cups flour. Bake in a quick oven.

3. 1 qt. molasses, 1 cup butter, ½ lb. sugar, spice to taste, and flour enough to roll.

4. 1 cup sweet milk or water, 2 do. sugar, ½ do. molasses, 1 do. butter or lard, 2 teaspoons ginger, 2 do. soda, flour enough to make the dough stiff to roll. Bake in a quick oven.

5. Melt together ¼ tin cup butter and lard mixed, ½ do. brown sugar, 1 do. baking molasses; then add 2 tablespoons ginger, 1 do. cloves, 2 teaspoons soda, enough flour to roll thin.

6. 1 pt. molasses, 1 teaspoon soda, 1 tablespoon ginger, butter the size of an egg. Knead hard and roll thin.

7. 1 cup Orleans molasses, 1 do. sugar, 1 egg, 1 tablespoon ginger, 1 do. vinegar, 1 large teaspoon soda, ½ cup butter, flour until stiff enough to roll.

8. 1 qt. molasses, 1 cup sour milk, 1 do. lard, 1 tablespoon ginger, 2 tablespoons soda, flour enough to roll and no more.

9. 1 qt. molasses, 1 pt. lard or butter, 2 cups sugar, ginger, cloves and cinnamon.

10. 1 pt. molasses, 1 small cup lard, 1 cup brown sugar, cloves to taste. Make stiff and roll thin.

11. 1½ cups molasses, ½ cup sugar, 1 do. butter, 1 teaspoon soda dissolved in ½ cup water. Ginger to taste, mix stiff and roll thin.

12. ½ cup ginger, 1 do. sugar, 1 do. molasses, 1 teaspoon soda, 1 cup butter. Flour enough to roll.

13. 1 qt. molasses, 1 pt. thick milk, ½ lb. lard, 3 tablespoons soda, 1½ tablespoons ginger.

14. 1 cup butter, 1 do. sugar, 2 do. molasses, 1 tablespoon soda dissolved in 1 cup water, 3 tablespoons ginger, mix very stiff.

15. 1 cup butter, 1 egg, 5 cups flour, 1 cup sweet milk, 2 do. sugar, 1 teaspoon soda. Flavor with lemon or cinnamon, and roll very thin.

16. 1 pint molasses, 2 cups sugar, 1 do. lard, 1 do. milk, ginger to taste. Knead stiff, roll thin, bake in tins.

17. 1 qt. Orleans molasses, ¾ tin sour milk, 2 tablespoons soda, 1 do. ginger, ¾ lb. lard. Flour enough to stiffen.

18. 1 pt. molasses, 1 cup sugar, ½ lb. butter, 6 eggs, beat the whites, 1 pt. sour milk, 1 oz. soda, 2½ lbs. flour, ginger enough to taste. Bake either in large or small cakes.

19. ¼ lb. butter, ¼ lb. lard, ¼ lb. brown sugar, 1 pt. molasses, 2 tablespoons ginger, 1 qt. flour, 1 cup sour milk, 2 teaspoons saleratus.

20. 2 pts. baking molasses, 1 pt. thick milk, ¾ pt. lard, 2 tablespoons soda, 2 do. ginger. To brown, make a wash of yolk of egg and water sweetened. Make into soft dough, roll and bake.

21. 1 pt. molasses, ½ lb. sugar, ½ do. lard, 2 tablespoons ginger, 1 tablespoon cloves, add sufficient flour to make the dough stiff enough to roll.

SUGAR PRETZELS.

1 cup sugar, 2 eggs, ½ cup butter, ½ teaspoon soda, flour to roll, and roll them in sugar.

SCOTCH CAKES.

1. 1 lb. brown sugar, 1 do. flour, ½ do. butter, 2 eggs, cinnamon, roll very thin.

2. 1 lb. flour, 1 do. brown sugar, ¼ do. butter, 4 eggs, a little soda and lemon oil, work the butter before adding the sugar and eggs. Let the flour be worked in lightly, having your dough as thin as you can work it when rolling out. Bake in a quick oven.

SAND CAKES.

1. 1 cup butter, 4 eggs, 1 lb. sugar, 1 cup milk, 6 cups flour, 1 teaspoon soda.

2. 1 cup butter, 2 do. sugar, 2 eggs, nutmeg and cinnamon. Make stiff, roll thin and bake in a slow oven.

3. 3 eggs, 1 lb. white sugar, 1 do. flour, ½ do. butter, work all together, roll out thin, cut in squares, wash with the yolk of an egg, sprinkle cinnamon, sugar and almond kernels over the top. Bake in quick oven.

4. 3 cups sugar, 1 do. butter, 3 eggs, beat the eggs, sugar and butter together until light, 6 cups flour, 1 do. sour cream, 1 teaspoon soda, 1 do. cream tartar, mix with the flour, and then mix all together. Roll out thin, sprinkle with sugar.

SNOW BALLS.

1 pt. sweet cream, 6 eggs, flour to make a stiff dough, then bake in lard.

DROP CAKES.

1. Whites of 2 eggs, beaten to a stiff froth, 2 oz. pulverized sugar, ½ lb. cocoanut, lemon, bake on buttered paper.

2. 1 pt. molasses, 4 eggs, 1 cup butter, 1 do. sugar, 1 tablespoon soda, 1 tablespoon cinnamon, 6 cups flour.

3. 1 lb. brown sugar, 4 eggs, 1 teaspoon soda, 2 do. cream tartar, spice to taste. Flour enough to drop in pans.

4. 4 cups sugar, 1 cup butter, 8 eggs, 1 cup sour cream, 2 teaspoons soda, 4 teaspoons cream tartar, 5 cups flour.

5. 5 cups flour, 2 do. sugar, 3 do. sour cream, 2 eggs, 4 teaspoons cream tartar, 1 do. soda, 2 tablespoons butter.

6. 1 pt. Orleans molasses, with 1 tablespoon dry soda beaten into the molasses until light, 1 cup lard, ½ pt. boiling water, 1 tablespoon ginger, and flour enough to make the drop.

7. 2 cups sugar, 2 do. sweet cream, 1 do. butter, 2 eggs, 2 teaspoons soda, flour enough to make a stiff batter.

8. 3 cups sugar, 4 eggs, 1 cup sour milk, 1 do. butter, 1 teaspoon soda, 2 do. cream tartar, nutmeg, 5 cups flour.

9. 1 lb. flour, 4 eggs, ¾ lb. sugar, ½ lb. butter, 1 pt. cream, 1 nutmeg, soda and nuts.

10. 1 lb. sugar, ¾ lb. butter, 1¼ lbs. flour, 5 eggs. Dropped on buttered pans and baked.

11. 1 lb. sugar, 4 eggs, 1 cup butter, 1 do. sour cream, 1 teaspoon soda, 1 do. cream tartar.

12. 1 lb. hickory nut kernels, fine, 1 lb. white sugar, 1 egg, whites of 5 eggs, 2 tablespoons flour, and bake on paper in a slow oven. This is for small drop cakes.

13. 1 lb. sugar, 1 qt. walnut kernels, the whites of 6 eggs, 8 tablespoons flour. Drop on tin pans.

14. 1 pt. baking molasses, 1 cup brown sugar, 1 do. buttermilk, 1 egg, 1 cup lard or butter, spice to suit your taste, 1 tablespoon soda dissolved in milk, put in last, flour to thicken. Drop with a spoon.

15. 5 cups flour, 2 do. sugar, 2 do. sour cream, 2 eggs, 4 teaspoons cream tartar, 2 do. soda, 2 do. butter.

BUNNS.

1. 2 eggs, 1 cup sugar, ½ do. butter, 1 do. sour cream, 1 teaspoon cream tartar, 1 do. soda, 2 cups flour. Spice.

2. 2 cups sugar, 2 eggs, 1 tablespoon butter, 1 teaspoon soda, 1 do. cream tartar, 3 cups flour. Buttermilk to make a batter.

3. 5 eggs, 1 lb. sugar, 1 cup butter, 1 pt. sweet milk, 1 teaspoon soda, 1 do. cream tartar, flour to stiffen, when done spread on the top cinnamon and sugar mixed together.

4. 3 cups flour, 2 eggs, 2 cups sugar, butter the size of a large walnut, 1 teaspoon cream tartar, buttermilk to make a thin batter.

5. 1 lb. flour, 1 lb. sugar, 4 eggs, 1 cup butter, 1½ do. milk, 1 teaspoon soda, 1 do. cream tartar. Cream the butter, then add the sugar, the yolks of the eggs and the milk, then the whites and the flour, put the soda in last, beat the whites separately.

DOUGHNUTS.

1. 2 cups sugar, 2 eggs, 1 cup sour cream, 1 teaspoon soda.

2. 2 cups white sugar, 1 do. sweet milk, 3 eggs, 1 tablespoon melted butter, 1 small teaspoon soda, 2 teaspoons cream tartar. Mix with flour as soft as they can be rolled out, and fry in lard.

3. 2 cups sugar, ½ do. butter, 1 do. sour milk, 3 eggs, 1 teaspoon soda, ½ nutmeg, bake in fat.

4. 1 lb. sugar, 5 eggs, 1 cup sour cream, ½ do. butter, bake in lard.

5. 2 cups sugar, 1 do. butter or lard, 3 eggs, 1 teaspoon soda, 2 teaspoons cream tartar, 1 pint sour milk.

6. 1 qt. buttermilk, ½ tin lard, 3 eggs, 2 cups sugar, stir in crock as stiff as you can, then put on the board and knead with as little flour as possible, 1 teaspoon soda, 2 teaspoons cream tartar.

7. ½ cup shortening, 1 do. sweet milk, 1½ do. sugar, 3 eggs, a heaping teaspoon soda, make it very stiff and roll thin. Bake in lard.

8. 2 cups sour milk, 1 do. white sugar, 6 tablespoons melted lard, 1 teaspoon salt, 1 do. soda. Enough flour to make stiff dough. Do not roll — twist.

9. 1 pt. of raised dough wet with milk, knead in a teacup of sifted sugar, 2 eggs and a heaping tablespoon of butter, let it rise again, roll and fry.

10. 1 qt. of butter milk, 2 cups sugar, 3 eggs, 1 pint of lard, 1 teaspoon of soda, 1 do. cream tartar.

KISSES.

Take the whites of 4 eggs, beat them very lightly and mix with them enough sifted sugar to make them very stiff, then drop on paper half the size you want them, put them in a slow oven twenty minutes, take them off the paper with a knife, put two together. 4 eggs make a cake basket full.

CREAM CAKE.

Whites of 9 eggs, beaten to a froth. To every white of an egg, grate the rinds of 2 lemons, shake in gently 1 spoonful of refined sugar. Lay a wet sheet of paper on a tin and drop the froth in little lumps on it, sift plenty of sugar over them and put in a moderate oven. As soon as slightly brown, lay them together by twos on a sieve and dry in a cool oven.

VANITY CAKE.

3 eggs, ½ teaspoon salt, and flour enough to make a stiff dough. Roll the thickness of a knife-blade, and fry in lard.

POTATO CAKES.

1 qt. mashed potatoes, 2 eggs, 1½ pts. sweet milk, lump of butter size of an egg, 1 tablespoon sugar, 2 tablespoons of flour. Fry in hot lard.

PUDDINGS.

QUEEN OF PUDDINGS.

1. 1 qt. milk, ⅜ pt. bread crumbs, the yolks of 5 eggs, well beaten, sweeten and flavor to taste. Bake until done but not watery, beat the whites to a stiff froth, adding some sugar, spread over the pudding a layer of jelly or any sweetmeats you prefer. Pour the whites over this, replace in the oven, and bake until the meringue is a light brown.

2. 1 pt. bread crumbs, 1 qt. sweet milk, ¾ cup sugar, 4 eggs, whites and yolks separately, butter the size of a walnut, 1 grated lemon, bake until done, then spread jelly on it, the whites beaten with sugar, put on the pudding, brown it, and serve with cream.

3. 1 qt. milk, 4 eggs, 1 pt. bread crumbs, beat the eggs separately, sugar to sweeten it; add to the beaten whites 4 tablespoons sugar, and spread on the top after it is baked; set it in the oven one minute to brown.

4. 1 pt. bread crumbs to 1 qt. milk, 1 cup sugar, the yolks of 4 eggs beaten, the grated rind of a lemon, butter the size of an egg, bake until done but not watery, whip the whites of the eggs stiff and beat in a teacup sugar in which has been stirred the juice of the lemon, spread over the pudding a layer of jelly, pour the whites of the eggs over this, and replace in the oven and bake lightly.

BREAD PUDDINGS.

1. 1 pt. fine bread crumbs to 1 qt. milk, 1 cup sugar, yolks of 4 eggs, well beaten, grated rind of 1 lemon, butter the size of an egg, don't let it bake until watery, whip the whites of the eggs with 1 teacup sugar, to a stiff froth, and put into this the juice of the lemon, spread over the pudding a layer of jelly, then spread the whites of eggs over this, and put in the oven and bake lightly.

2. 1 pt. fine bread crumbs, 1 qt. milk, 4 eggs, 2 cups sugar, butter the size of a walnut, beat the whites of the eggs and 1 cup of sugar to a stiff froth and put on the top, brown lightly. Lemon to taste.

3. This saves dry pieces of bread. It must be wheat. Take about the same as 2 slices of bread, soak in sweet milk until the bread is soft. Then mash it in the milk, so that the bread may be very fine; add 2 eggs well beaten, and sweet milk enough to fill your dish, which should hold about 2 qts., sweeten and spice, put in a little salt and a little butter. Put in the oven and bake.

4. 1 cup sugar, 2 do. bread crumbs, 4 eggs, 1 tablespoon cornstarch, 1 qt. sweet milk, spice with nutmeg. Rice can be used instead of bread if preferred.

5. 3 pts. bread dough, after it is raised, 2 eggs, 1 cup sugar, ½ do. lard, roll out and have 1 pt. stewed apples spread over, roll up and cook in a poke in water half an hour. Eat with cream and sugar.

RICE PUDDINGS.

1. Put into a pudding dish 1 cup rice, 1 qt. sweet milk, 1 teaspoon salt, 1 tablespoon white sugar, 1 teaspoon butter. Bake slowly.

2. 1 qt. milk, 3 eggs, 4 tablespoons sugar, 1 do. butter, 2 teaspoons lemon, 1 pt. rice.

3. 3 tablespoons rice, 5 do. sugar, a piece of butter as large as a hickory nut and a little salt. Let the rice boil up three or four times in a gill or more of water, then stir in the sugar, butter and salt, and add 1 qt. of milk, boil one hour. Let it get cold, grate nutmeg over it and serve.

4. ¼ lb. rice boiled and allowed to get cold, ¼ lb. sugar, ¼ lb. butter, 6 eggs, 1½ pts. new milk, a little salt. Mix the rice when cold with sugar and milk. The whites of eggs to be beaten separately and added last. Bake in an oven not too hot.

SUET PUDDING.

1. 4 cups flour, 1 cup molasses, 1 cup suet, 1 cup sweet milk, 1 cup raisins, 1 teaspoon soda. Mix, and boil 3 hours. Any kind of spice.

2. 3 cups flour, 1 cup suet, 1 cup chopped raisins, 1 cup Orleans molasses, 1 teaspoon soda dissolved in warm water, steam 3 hours. Dressing of butter, flour, sugar, vanilla and boiling water.

COTTAGE PUDDING.

1. 3 cups flour, 1 cup sugar, 1 cup milk, 2 tablespoons melted butter, 2 teaspoons cream tartar, 1 egg. Mix all together, then add 1 teaspoon soda. Flavor with lemon, bake ½ hour, and serve with sauce.

Sauce for Cottage Pudding.—1 cup butter and 2 cups powdered sugar beaten to a cream, 1 tablespoon vanilla, ½ pt. boiling water.

2. 1 pt. flour, 1 cup milk, 1 egg, 1 cup sugar, 1 teaspoon soda dissolved in the milk, 2 teaspoons cream tartar, bake ½ hour. Eat with cream and sugar.

TAPIOCA PUDDING.

1. 1 qt. milk, ¾ teacup tapioca, soaked in a pint of the milk over night. In the morning stir in the other pint with 4 eggs well beaten, sweeten to taste and flavor with lemon; bake until done, and eat cold.

2. Soak 4 tablespoons of tapioca in water over night. 1 qt. of milk, yolks of 4 eggs, 1 grated lemon, sweeten to taste. Bake 1 hour. Beat whites of eggs with 4 tablespoons of sugar for frosting. Pour on pudding and brown slightly. Good.

MISCELLANEOUS PUDDINGS.

BIRD'S NEST PUDDING.—Take 8 or 10 ripe apples, take out the cores leaving them whole, prepare a custard, 6 eggs to 1 qt. milk, flavor with lemon or nutmeg, lay the apples in a pudding dish, pour the custard over them and bake ½ hour.

MINUTE PUDDING.—Put 1 qt. of milk over a clear fire, 1 teacup flour with cold milk enough to make a smooth batter, add 1 teaspoon salt, when the milk boils stir in the batter gradually until it thickens, boil gently for a few minutes, pour into your mould when cold, serve with cream or wine sauce.

EGG PUDDING.—3 eggs, 3 pints sweet milk, a little salt, 1 pint dried apples cut fine and flour enough to make a stiff batter, pour into a greased pan, and bake ½ hour in a quick oven. To be served hot, with sweet milk.

APPLE TAPIOCA PUDDING.—Pour 1 qt. boiling water over 4 tablespoons tapioca. Let boil until clear, then add 1 tablespoon melted butter, 4 large apples pared and sliced, 2 teaspoons vanilla, orange or lemon, sweeten to taste. Let it boil until the apples begin to soften, then bake in an oven ½ hour. To be eaten cold with cream.

CREAM TAPIOCA PUDDING.—Soak 3 tablespoons tapioca in water over night, pour it into one qt. boiling milk, then boil ten minutes; beat the yolks of 4 eggs with 1 cup sugar and 1 tablespoon prepared cocoanut, stir in and boil 5 minutes longer, then pour into a white pudding dish. Beat the whites of the eggs to a froth, and add 3 tablespoons sugar, pour over the pudding, and sprinkle over the top the prepared cocoanut. Set in the oven and brown 5 minutes.

FAYETTE PUDDING.—Slice stale bread, lay the slices in the bottom of a dish, cutting them so as to cover it completely, sprinkle sugar and nutmeg, with a little butter on each layer and when all are in, pour on 1 qt. rich boiling custard, and serve cold.

LEMON PUDDING.—Grate the rind of 2 lemons, squeeze in the juice, grate ½ dozen water crackers, ¾ lb. sugar, yolks of 12 eggs and the whites of 6, ¾ lb. melted butter, ½ pint thick cream. Mix all well together. Lay puff paste in your dish and bake.

POTATO PUDDING.—1 lb. sugar, ¾ lb. butter, 10 eggs, whites beaten to a froth; 1 lb. potatoes, boiled and mashed through a sieve; ¾ wineglass rosewater, ½ nutmeg, grated.

FLOAT.—Mix the beaten yolks of 4 eggs with 1 tablespoon corn starch, add flavor and stir into 1 qt. boiling milk, let it boil a few minutes, pour into a dish and spread over the top the whites of the eggs well beaten, sweeten with white sugar.

GERMAN PUFFS.—1 pt. milk, butter the size of an egg melted in the milk, 3 eggs, a little salt, and flour to make a very thin batter. Bake in cups and serve with sweetened cream.

MOLASSES PUDDING.—1 cup baking molasses, 1 cup water, 3 cups flour, ½ cup melted butter, 1 teaspoon soda, steam 3 hours, 1 egg, equal quantities of butter and sugar, beaten light for dressing.

KISS OR DANDY PUDDING.—1 qt. milk, put over steam to scald, when scalded stir in the yolks of 4 eggs, 1 cup sugar, 3 tablespoons corn starch, boil till quite thick, then pour in an earthen dish and bake. When done spread over this the whites of the eggs, and brown slightly.

STEAM PUDDING.—1 qt. flour, 1 cup chopped raisins or currants, 1 teacup chopped suet, ½ cup molasses, finish with brown sugar, 1 teaspoon soda, 2 cups sweet milk, with a little salt. Mix and steam three hours. Sauce.

FIG PUDDING.—½ lb. finely-chopped figs, 1 cup suet, 1 do. brown sugar, 1 heaping cup bread crumbs, 2 eggs, ½ teaspoon soda, 1 teaspoon cream tartar, 2 tablespoons brandy. Flavor with nutmeg and cinnamon. Steam 3 hours.

PUDDING SAUCE.—Melt in a stewpan 2 oz. butter, add 2 tablespoons flour, (arrow root would probably be better,) some milk, hot water and sugar. Boil; add when on the table, essence of lemon, nutmeg, and brandy.

BATTER PUDDING.—Put in a dish some good baking apples cut up fine, pour over them a batter made of 4 tablespoons flour, 4 eggs, 1 pt. milk; fit a buttered floured cloth over the dish, boil 1 hour, turn out on a hot dish. Eat with sugar and cream.

CORN-STARCH PUDDING.—3 tablespoons corn starch, 1 qt. milk, 4 eggs, grate nutmeg on when cold. To be eaten with sugar and cream, flavored with lemon or vanilla.

APPLE CITRON.—To 3 tincups bread, boiled, and mashed apples, add 1 tin sugar; boil until stiff. Lemon to taste.

ENGLISH PUDDING.—Beat lightly the yolks of 10 eggs, and the whites of 6, with ¾ lb. sugar, the rind of an orange or two lemons grated, 6½ oz. flour, 1 pt. boiling milk. When nearly cold, mix in the eggs and sugar, and add a wineglass of brandy and ½ lb. melted butter. Bake one hour and a half.

SNOWDEN PUDDING.—½ lb. bread crumbs, ½ lb. suet, ½ lb. moist sugar, rind and juice of 2 lemons, 3 eggs, boil 2 hours and serve with wine sauce.

TYLER PUDDING.—3 cups brown sugar, 1 cup butter, 1 qt. sweet milk, 4 eggs. Beat the butter, sugar, and yolks together as for cake, then put in the milk. Have the whites beat light and put in last. Season with lemon and bake as for custards. Very rich.

CHARLOTTE RUSSE PUDDING.—Boil 1 qt. milk, stir in slowly the yolks of 6 eggs well beaten, sweeten and flavor; when cool, slice in ¼ lb. sponge cake, beat the whites of the eggs to a stiff froth, and add 6 tablespoons white sugar, lay this over the custard. Bake 10 or 15 minutes.

ORANGE PUDDING.—Cut 6 oranges fine, and sugar them. Make a custard of 4 eggs, 1 qt. milk, 2 tablespoons cornstarch. When cool, pour the custard over the oranges.

WELSH PUDDING.—Scald two pints of bread crumbs, then put in 1 good handful flour, ½ cup sugar, a lump of butter the size of a small egg, a few raisins, knead it, and boil in cloths. For dressing, take a few tablespoons of flour and mix the same as for chicken dressing. Then take boiling water, stir the flour into it, a little sugar and some butter, a few spoonfuls of vinegar, season with nutmeg or cinnamon.

CREAMS, CUSTARDS, ETC.

VELVET CREAMS.

1. 1 qt. cream, the yolk of 1 egg and the whites of 3, well beaten, sweeten and flavor to taste, dissolve 1 oz. gelatine in 1 cup warm milk; stir all together, pour into a mould, and when it congeals it is ready for use. This is nice eaten with cream.

2. 1 qt. sweet cream, whipped, ¼ box Cox's gelatine dissolved in warm water, 1 wineglass wine or brandy. Sweeten to the taste.

LEMON CUSTARDS.

1. 1 lemon, 3 eggs, 1 cup sugar, 1½ pts. sweet milk, 2 tablespoons butter, 2 do. flour.

2. 1 large or 2 small lemons, (for two pies,) grate the lemons, and put in the juice also, 1 cup water, 1 do. sugar, the yolks of 4 eggs, beaten, 2 grated crackers; mix the water, sugar, and lemon, then add the eggs and crackers. When the pies are baked, have the whites of the eggs beaten stiff and sweetened, then spread over the pies, and put them in the oven to brown.

3. 1 large lemon, 4 eggs, 2 tablespoons corn starch, 1 qt. sweet milk, lump butter the size of an egg. Sweeten to taste.

4. 2 cups sugar, 4 eggs, 1 lemon, 3 cups water, 2 tablespoons flour. Beat the yolks with the sugar, and the whites separate; stir the whites in just before putting in the oven. Bake until a light brown.

PUMPKIN CUSTARDS.

1. 1 pt. boiled pumpkin, press in a cloth to get all the water out, yolks of 4 eggs, 2 tablespoons flour mixed smoothly with milk, 1 qt. sweet milk, a little butter. Sweeten to taste.

2. 1 pt. boiled pumpkin, add ¼ lb. butter, 1 teacup sugar, 2 tablespoons flour, 1 qt. milk, 1 grated nutmeg, and 4 eggs beaten separately. Stir the yolks thoroughly into the mixture, and add the whites, beating lightly just before putting on the paste.

MISCELLANEOUS CUSTARDS, CREAMS, &C.

BUTTERMILK CUSTARD.—1 qt. buttermilk, 4 eggs, 2 cups sugar, 1 do. flour, 1 teaspoon soda. Flavor with lemon or nutmeg.

POTATO CUSTARD.—Boil 1 lb. fine potatoes, mash and rub them through a colander, stir together to a cream, ¾ lb. sugar, and ¼ lb. butter, flavor with nutmeg. Beat 6 eggs very light, and add them by degrees to the mixture alternately with the potatoes. Bake as other custards.

FROZEN CUSTARD.—Boil 1 qt. milk with cinnamon and a few peach leaves, say about a dozen; beat 6 eggs well and mix them in the milk after it is boiled, adding, also, a teaspoon of cornstarch. Sweeten the milk according to your liking and pour it into an iron pan, stirring it well one way; then give the custard a simmer until it has the proper thickness, but do not let it boil. It must be stirred one way all the time. If preferred, ½ cream and ½ milk may be used.

FLOAT.—6 eggs to 1 qt. milk; beat the whites separately, the yellow and ½ cup sugar; boil the whites and the milk a few minutes, then stir the yellows in; merely boil, stiring all the time.

APPLE CREAM.—6 large apples stewed and mashed, sweeten to taste, the whites of 4 eggs beaten to a froth, then beat in with apples. Serve with cream.

COCOANUT CUSTARD.—1 qt. milk, 5 eggs, 1 grated cocoanut, beat the eggs and sugar together, (sugar to taste,) stir in the milk and some ground cinnamon. Bake in a bottom crust, mix the cocoanut with some sugar, and lay on the top; put in the oven until it commences to brown.

VANILLA CREAM.—½ box Cox's gelatine dissolved in 1 pt. cold water, put in the whites of 4 eggs, without beating, a small cup of sugar, and flavor strongly with vanilla. Beat all until light. Eaten with cream.

CHARLOTTE RUSSE.—To ½ pt. milk, put a little over ½ oz. isinglass, and flavor to taste. Put to simmer over fire, beat the whites of 4 eggs to a stiff froth, stir the yolks with 3 oz. sugar, beat 1 pt. thick cream and 1 wineglass wine to a complete froth. When the isinglass is dissolved, strain the milk while warm into the yolks and sugar, then add the cream, beat lightly together, and pour over the cake. Sponge cake the best. Any kind of wine will do.

ROGARD.—Take 1 qt. fruit that is juicy, put 1 qt. water on it and let it cook until quite soft, then strain off all the liquid and put where it will boil. Mix 3 tablespoons cornstarch with water, and as soon as it boils stir it in and sweeten to taste. It looks very pretty when put in moulds to cool.

Line the sides and bottom of the dish with sponge cake, pare some ripe peaches, cut them in halves, sprinkle with sugar, fill the dish, whip sweetened cream to a froth and pour over.

STRAWBERRY ICE CREAM.—1 pt. mashed fruit, ¼ lb. sugar, 1 pt. cream, and freeze.

APPLE SNOW.—Pare and core 12 large apples, stew them perfectly soft, add ½ lb. sugar, and rub the apples through a fine seive, stir into it the beaten yolks of 2 eggs and grated peel of a lemon, beat it for five minutes. Beat the whites of the eggs to a stiff froth. Put the apples into a glass dish and heap the whites over it.

BUTTERMILK CUSTARD.—1 pt. buttermilk, 2 eggs, 1 tablespoon flour, 2 tablespoons sugar, add cinnamon and salt.

APPLE CUSTARD.—Take sour apples, stew till soft and not much water left in them, then rub through a colander. Beat 3 eggs for each pie to be baked. Put 1 cup butter, 3 cups sugar for four pies. Flavor to taste.

SNOW BALLS.—Swell rice in milk, pare and core your apples, put the rice around them, put a little lemon peel, cloves and cinnamon in each, tie each in a cloth and boil them. To be served with sweetened cream.

GELATINE.—1 box gelatine soaked in 1 pt. of cold water an hour, with 2 lemons, and then add 3 pts. boiling water, 1½ lbs. sugar, stir well, and then strain. As soon as cold, ready for use.

ORANGE DESSERT.—Take ½ doz. sweet oranges, peel and cut in small pieces, grate a nice fresh cocoanut, and sugar both together. To be eaten with cream.

POTATO CUSTARD.—1 cup sugar, 1 do. hot water, 2 raw potatoes grated, 2 eggs, and a small quantity of flour.

PIES.

LEMON PIES.

1. 1 grated lemon, 1 cup sugar, 1 do. water, 1 beaten egg, 1 tablespoon flour, 2 tablespoons sweet cream.

2. Scald 1 pt. milk, beat well the yolks of 4 eggs, roll 6 crackers fine, 1 cup sugar, juice and grated rind of 1 lemon, stir all together in the milk and add a little cold milk, beat the whites of eggs and ¼ cup sugar to a stiff froth. When the pie is baked and cold, spread this over the top and return it to the oven and brown.

3. 1 lemon, 1 cup sugar, the yolks of 3 eggs, 2 tablespoons flour, ½ cup water. Take the whites of the 3 eggs and 3 tablespoons sugar and beat to a froth, and then turn it over the pie when baked. Set it in the oven again and let it remain 3 minutes. Use but one crust.

4. WM. D. GOBRECHT'S FAVORITE LEMON PIE.—Chop your lemon fine, use the rind and all except the seeds; then to each lemon take 2 eggs, ½ cup sugar, ½ cup molasses, add 1 cup water to every 4 lemons and stir in a tablespoon flour, or arrow root starch. Make a nice paste and bake with 2 crusts.—Jan. 24, 1858.

5. To 1 lemon take 1 lb. sugar, 3 eggs, 2 tablespoons flour, 1 cup vinegar, 3 cups water. Bake in double crust.

6. 1 grated lemon, 1 cup sugar, 1 cup water, 2 grated crackers, 1 egg, to each pie add a small pinch of salt.

LEMON CUSTARD.

1. 1 grated lemon, 1 teacup sweet milk, 1 cup sugar, 1 tablespoon melted butter, 1 tablespoon flour, the yolks of 4 eggs, well beaten. Beat the whites to a stiff froth with 1 cup sugar, when the pies are just done, pour it over the top and brown lightly.

2. Take the whites of 1 egg and the yolks of 4, beat them well and pour over 2 teacups of brown sugar, stir all well together, then grate the rind and squeeze the juice of a good sized lemon in the sugar and eggs as above mixed and stir again, then take a heaping spoonful flour and mix it very smoothly with 2 tablespoons water, afterward thin it with $\frac{1}{2}$ spoonful water, then mix it with the rest, adding 2 teacups pure cold water and a pinch of salt. After lining the pie pans beat the whites of 3 eggs to a stiff froth and stir rapidly into the mixture, pour into the pans and bake a good $\frac{1}{2}$ hour, or a little longer if the oven is not very hot.

3. 1 large lemon, 2 cups sugar, 2 cups water, $\frac{1}{2}$ cup butter, 1 tablespoon flour, 3 eggs, beat the whites separately and put in last.

PIE CRUST FOR LEMON CUSTARD.—Take 3 good handfuls of flour, a pinch of salt and 2 tablespoons lard, with a piece of butter the size of an egg, mixing the lard well through the flour, and afterward the butter though not so thoroughly, in order that the crust might be more flaky, and then adding a very little cold water, just enough to make the dough adhere. It should be made as stiff as possible, lightly handled, not kneading it in the least, but rather squeezing it together; when rolling it touch the roller very lightly and do not turn the crust over.

GOLDEN PIES.

1. 1 cup sugar, 1 cup sweet milk, 4 eggs, whites beaten separately, $\frac{1}{2}$ cup sugar added and browned over the top, 1 lemon, grate $\frac{1}{2}$ the rind.

2. 1 lemon, grate the rind, squeeze the juice and pulp, remove the seeds, add 1 cup sweet milk, 1 cup sugar, 1 tablespoon butter, 1 tablespoon flour, yolks of 4 eggs, well beaten. Pour this mixture into a nice paste crust, and bake slowly. Beat the whites of 4 eggs to a stiff froth, and sweeten. When the pie is just done, pour over the top and put back in the oven till a nice brown.

3. 1 lemon, 1 cup sweet milk, $\frac{1}{2}$ cup sugar. Take the yolks of 4 eggs, with 1 cup sugar for the icing.

MINCE PIES.

1. 1 cup milk, 4 eggs, 1 cup vinegar, 1 cup sugar, 3 tablespoons flour, 1 teaspoon soda, 2 teaspooons cloves, 2 teaspoons cinnamon, 1 pint raisins.

2. 1 lb. meat, ½ lb. suet, 2½ lbs. apples, 2 lbs. raisins, 6 oz. citron, ½ tablespoon cloves, ½ tablespoon mace, 1 tablespoon cinnamon, ½ tablespoon salt, ½ nutmeg, 1 qt. cider, 2 lbs. sugar, ½ pint brandy.

MOCK MINCE PIES.—1 cup bread crumbs, 1 cup vinegar, 1 cup raisins, 1 cup water, 1 cup sugar, 1 cup molasses, ½ cup butter, 1 teaspoon cloves, 1 nutmeg, 1 teaspoon cinnamon.

PATENT MINCE PIE.—1 cup molasses, 1 cup sugar, 1 cup flour, 1 cup vinegar, 4 cups water, 4 eggs, 1 tablespoon ground cinnamon, 1 teaspoon cloves, 1 teaspoon soda.

MINCE PIE WITHOUT MEAT.—1 pt. sweet apples, chopped fine, ½ pt. sweet cream, 2 eggs, 1 cup raisins. Spice as for mince, and bake slow.

CRUMB PIES.

1. 1 cup sugar, 1 cup thick milk, 1 cup lard, 4 cups flour, 2 eggs, 1 teaspoon soda, 1 teaspoon cream tartar.

2. 5 cups flour, 2 cups sugar, 1 cup lard, 1 cup sour milk, 1 teaspoon soda, 1 teaspoon cream tartar.

3. 3 cups sugar, 1 cup butter, 4 cups flour, 1¼ cups sour milk, 3 eggs, 1 teaspoon soda, 1 teaspoon cream tartar.

SUGAR PIES.

1. 2 cups sugar, 1 pt. sour or sweet cream, 1 teaspoon soda, ½ do. cream tartar, 1 cup lard or butter, make it stiff enough to roll out.

2. 3 cups sugar, 2 eggs, 1½ cups sour milk, 1 cup lard, 1 teaspoon soda.

3. 5 cups flour, 2 do. sugar, 1 cup sour milk, 1 do. butter or lard, 1 teaspoon saleratus, 2 teaspoons cream tartar. To be made without crust.

MISCELLANEOUS.

CREAM PIE.—1 cup sweet cream, 1 do. sugar, 2 eggs, ½ cup vinegar, season with lemon or nutmeg. Bake in 2 crusts.

OYSTER PIE.—100 large oysters, 6 eggs boiled hard and chopped fine, a slice of stale bread grated fine, a tablespoon spice, (cloves and mace,) 1 tablespoon salt, 1 do. pepper. Butter the edge of the pan and put the paste around the sides of it, but not on the bottom. Pour in the oysters, then the spice, bread and eggs on the top. Bake one or one and a half hours.

GINGER PIE.—1 pt. molasses, 1 pt. buttermilk, ½ pt. lard, 1 tablespoon soda, 1 do. ginger, a little burnt alum.

SWEET POTATO PIE.—1 lb. sweet potatoes, boiled and rubbed through a sieve, ½ lb. butter, ½ lb. sugar, 1 qt. milk, 7 eggs, beaten separately, warm the butter, milk and other ingredients. Nutmeg and brandy to taste.

SHOO FLY PIE.—1 cup molasses, 1 do. boiling water, 1 teaspoon soda, 1 do. cream tartar, then take 3 cups flour, ½ cup lard, rub in crumbs, and stir them into the molasses, leave a few out to put on the top of the pies.

STRAWBERRY SHORT CAKE.—2 cups sour cream, 1 teaspoon soda, ½ teacup fresh butter, flour to make a batter the consistency of griddle-cake batter. Bake in jelly-cake tins. Beat 1 cup sweet cream, with which spread on each cake, covering with strawberries and sugar. Serve with sweet cream.

PUMPKIN PIE.—1 cup grated pumpkin, 1 pt. good milk or cream, 1 egg, a little salt, 2 large spoons sugar. Spice to taste.

VINEGAR PIE.—1 cup sugar, ½ cup vinegar, boil together and skim, when cool add 1 well beaten egg, stir briskly until the egg is all in, 1 large teaspoon butter, 1 heaped do. soda crackers, if no crackers, a bit of the pie baked and rolled will do. ½ teaspoon ground cloves for 1 pie.

DELICATE PIE.—The grated rind and juice of a lemon, 1 cup powdered sugar, the yolks of 3 eggs, 2 tablespoons flour, ⅔ cup water. Take the whites of 3 eggs and 3 tablespoons sugar, beat to a froth, and put it over the pie when baked. Set it in the oven again, and let it remain 3 minutes. Use but one crust.

BERRY OR FRUIT SHORT CAKE.—1 qt. flour, 1 teaspoon salt, 2 teaspoons Royal baking powder, 2 tablespoons butter, 1 pt. milk. Sift flour, salt and powder together, rub in butter cold, add the milk and mix just soft enough to handle. Roll out and bake on greased pans. Then endeavor to separate without cutting. Have the fruit sugared; spread on the bottom half of short cake, lay the top half with the crust down, cover with fruit. Thus for several layers, and serve with cream.

SPICE PIE.—1 cup sugar, 1 do. molasses, 1 do. flour, 4 cups water, 4 eggs, 1 teaspoon soda, 1 do. cinnamon, 1 do. cloves.

QUINCE TARTS.—Stew 6 quinces and strain, mix with them ½ lb. sugar, ½ pt. cream, 4 eggs, nutmeg to taste.

MOLASSES PIE.—1 cup sugar, 1 do. molasses, 1 do. milk, 1 do. butter, 4 cups flour, 2 tablespoons ginger, 1 teaspoon soda. Beat the soda and molasses together until it foams.

CREAM CUSTARD PIE.—1 cup sweet cream well beaten, 1 do. white sugar. Flavor with lemon. Bake a crust on a plate, when cold add the custard, dropping here and there a little apple jelly. This will make 4 pies.

SHOO FLY PIE—EXCELLENT.—1 cup molasses, 1 do. boiling water, 1 teaspoon soda, 1 do. ginger, mix well. Then mix well in separate pan, 3 cups flour, 1 cup sugar, ½ do. lard. Mix the two batters together thoroughly and bake in patty-pans without crust.

EGGS.

OMELETS.

1. 6 eggs, ½ pt. sweet milk, 2 tablespoons flour. Beat the eggs light, put in a pan, set on the stove, let it cook five minutes, stirring all the time, then put into the oven and bake fifteen minutes. Eat hot.

2. 1 cup new milk, 6 eggs, 1 tablespoon flour. Take the whites and beat them to a stiff froth, then stir them lightly together, then have a pan hot buttered, pour the batter in the pan, and bake in a quick oven.

3. Mix the yolks of 6 eggs, well beaten, with one cup sweet milk, 1 teaspoon salt, 1 tablespoon corn starch. Stir in slowly the whites of the eggs beaten to a froth, pour the whole into a hot skillet, in which you have placed a piece of butter the size of a walnut. It will take from ten to fifteen minutes to cook through. When done, run a knife through the side of the skillet to loosen the omelet, then quickly turn over on a large plate.

4. 5 eggs, 1 pt. milk, 2 tablespoons flour. Beat the eggs separately. Bake in a quick oven.

5. Take 7 eggs, beat them well, 1 teaspoon salt, some pepper, 1 pt. new milk, 3 tablespoons flour or bread crumbs. Grease the pan well, and bake brown.

OMELET WITH DRIED BEEF.—Chip your beef fine, and break into it 3 or 4 eggs, and a little salt. When the beef is heated, put in your eggs, and stir a few minutes.

APPLE OMELET.—8 large apples, 4 eggs, 1 cup sugar, 1 tablespoon butter, nutmeg or cinnamon to taste; stew the apples and mash fine, then add the butter and sugar; when cold add the eggs, well beaten; bake until brown. Eat while warm.

RUFFLED EGGS.—Take 4 large smooth eggs, pare them and gash the edges, then plunge for a moment into warm water, and separate the whites from the yolks; beat the whites briskly with a two-pronged fork until they assume of themselves a beautiful ruffled shape. Arrange the yolks in the centre of the dish, garnishing the edges with the ruffled whites; season plentifully with peppermint, and serve ice cold.

SNOW BALLS.—Take 6 eggs, 1 cup cream, flour to make them quite stiff, roll them out and cut with a whirl, bake them in lard, and grate loaf sugar over them when cold.

BREAD.

RUSKS.

1. 1 lb. butter, 1 lb. sugar, 1 qt. new milk, yeast to make it light; stir in enough of flour to make as thick as bread dough. When raised, work in a loaf and let it raise again, then put them in pans and let them stand half an hour before baking.

2. To 1 qt. of new milk take 1 pt. of good hop yeast, put in flour to make a batter; let it stand over night. In the morning put in 4 eggs, 1 lb. sugar, and a little lard, and when light bake in a quick oven.

3. Fill a large sized bowl with bread dough, ½ cup melted butter or lard, 2 eggs, ½ cup sugar, work out in pans, and bake in a quick oven, after raising very light.

4. 1 cup lard, 1 pt. milk, 1 cup sugar, 1 cup yeast, 2 eggs, and a little nutmeg.

5. 1 cup sweet milk, 1 do. yeast, 2 do. sugar, 3 eggs; let raise before cutting out.

BISCUIT.

POUNDED BISCUIT.—1 qt. flour, ½ cup butter or lard, make a stiff dough with water; work and beat till soft. Stick with a fork and bake in a quick oven.

AMERICAN BISCUIT.—Rub ½ lb. butter into 4 lbs. of flour, add a full pt. of milk or water; beat them well. Break your dough well, and bake in a hot oven.

TEA BISCUIT.—1 pt. flour, 1 cup butter, 1 pt. of sweet milk, 3 teaspoons cream tartar stirred in the flour, 1 teaspoon soda, and a little salt.

SUGAR BISCUIT.—2½ cups sugar, 1 large cup sweet milk, 1 cup shortening, 1 teaspoon soda, 1 do. cream tartar in the milk, 2 eggs, flour to stiffen. Sprinkle each cake with sugar before baking.

CREAM BISCUIT.—1 qt. flour, 1 cup good buttermilk, 1 do. tolerably thick sour cream, 1 small teaspoon salt, 1½ teaspoons soda. Roll out ¾ of an inch in thickness.

POTATO BISCUIT.—1 pt. mashed potatoes, ¾ cup lard or butter, 3 eggs, 1 cup sugar, 1 qt. flour, 1 cup yeast; let it rise till morning, put flour in to make it stiff enough, add 2 teaspoons of baking powder. Cut into cakes, let rise, and then bake in a quick oven.

HARD TIMES BISCUIT.— 3 pts. flour, ¾ cup lard or butter, 1 pt. sweet milk, 2 teaspoons baking powder. Bake in a quick oven.

SODA BISCUITS.

1. Take 3 tin cups flour, 1 tin cup lard, 1 tin cup sweet milk, 1 teaspoon soda, 2 teaspoons cream tartar.

2. Take 1 qt. of flour, 1 lump butter size of a walnut, 1 teaspoon cream tartar, 1 teaspoon soda dissolved in a little boiling water, put into a pint sour milk, as little flour as possible. Bake in a quick oven. Very good.

3. 3 pints flour, 1 teaspoon soda, 3 tablespoons lard or butter, 1 teaspoon salt, buttermilk enough to make a soft dough. Bake in a quick oven.

CORN BREAD.

1. Take 1 qt. corn meal, 2 eggs, 1 tablespoon yeast powder, a little salt and milk, enough to make a batter as thick as for sweet cakes, bake as soon as mixed up. Make corn cakes the same way, only make the batter much thinner.

2. 2 cups corn meal, 2 cups wheat flour, ½ cup lard or ham drippings, ¼ cup sugar, 4 eggs, 2 cups milk, 1 of sour and 1 of sweet; 2 teaspoons soda, 2 do. cream tartar. Add whites of eggs last, and bake in an earthen dish one hour.

3. Take 3 cups of thick cream, 2 eggs, 1 teaspoon salt and 1 of soda, butter about the size of a hen's egg; mix together with Indian meal sufficient to make a batter. Bake in a hot oven.

4. 1 pt. corn meal, 1 do. sour milk, ½ cup butter, 1 teaspoon soda, 2 eggs, a little wheat flour. Bake in a dish.

5. 1 pt. of sour milk, 1 do. of corn meal, 3 eggs, 2 tablespoons sugar, small piece of butter, 1 teaspoon saleratus or soda. Enough for 3 pie tins.

6. 1 qt. milk, 1 pt. Indian meal, 3 eggs, ¼ lb. butter. Boil the milk and with it scald the Indian meal, stir it gradually, the meal and butter. When cool add the eggs. Bake in square tins, half an inch of batter when put in pans.

7. 1 pt. corn meal scalded, ¼ lb. of shortening put into the meal while hot, salt to taste. 1 cup thick milk, 1 egg, 2 teaspoons soda. Bake ½ hour in a quick oven.

CORN BATTER CAKES.—1 pt. corn meal, pour boiling water over it, let it stand to cool, thin with milk or water, a little salt, a small teaspoon of soda, 2 eggs, beat the whites and put in just before baking.

CORN CAKES TO EAT WHEN WARM.—1 pt. sour milk, 2 cups Indian meal, 1 cup flour, 1 egg, 2 tablespoons of molasses, a little salt, 1 teaspoon soda, mix thoroughly and bake twenty-five minutes in 2 pans.

WAFFLES.

1. Take 1 pt. of sour cream, 1½ pts. sweet milk, 4 eggs, 1 teaspoon of soda.

2. 1 pt. new milk, the yolks of 4 beaten eggs stirred in the milk and afterwards the whites, ¼ lb. butter melted and stirred in, a little salt, 1 teaspoon soda dissolved in milk and strained, nearly all the flour, 1 pt. sour cream and sufficient flour to make the batter as stiff as pound cake. Serve as soon as baked. Grease the irons with sweet butter, serve with pulverized loaf sugar, and strong cinnamon, ground and sifted.

3. 1 qt. of warm milk, 5 large cups of flour, 3 eggs, ⅔ cup of yeast, a little salt, set as a sponge, 2 tablespoons butter. Irons hot and well greased with lard.

GOOD WAFFLES.—1 qt. sour milk, 1 egg, 1 teaspoon soda, 1 tablespoon butter, 1 tablespoon sugar, flour to make as for griddle cakes.

SWEET WAFFLES.—½ cup butter, 2 cups sugar, 3 cups flour, 3 eggs, ½ cup milk, ½ teaspoon soda, 1 teaspoon cream tartar.

SNAP BUCKWHEAT CAKES.—1 qt. buttermilk, or cream, which is better, 1 teaspoon bicarbonate soda, 1 teaspoon salt. Sufficient buckwheat flour to stiffen. Stir until mixed and no longer. Turn before baked through, but not more than once. Pop the cakes under a cover immediately to steam.

CHEAP FLANNEL CAKES.—To 1 pint of thick milk take a little salt, ½ teaspoon soda and flour enough to make a thin batter. No eggs called for. Splendid for breakfast.

APPLE FRITTERS.—Make a batter as for plain fritters, pare and grate 5 good sized apples, and stir into the batter, add the grated rind of a lemon, or nutmeg.

CORN PONE.

1. 2 cups Indian meal, 1 cup flour, 2 cups sour milk, ¾ cup sugar, 2 eggs, ½ teaspoon soda. Butter the size of a walnut.

2. Take 4 eggs, 1 pt. sour cream, 1 teaspoon soda, 1 tablespoon sugar, corn meal sufficient to make a thick batter. Bake one hour and serve while hot.

3. 6 eggs, 1 qt. sweet milk, small lump of butter warmed, 1 teaspoon salt, 1 do. soda, 2 do. sugar, 1½ pts. corn meal. Bake in buttered tins.

MUFFINS.

POTATO MUFFINS.—2 tincups mashed potatoes, scant cup of lard, 1 cup of yeast, knead very stiff. If they are to be baked for breakfast they must be put in the pans the night before, cut about an inch thick. In cool weather they can be kept for several days by working them down once a day, which improves them.

VANITIES.—Beat 3 eggs, put in a little salt, add flour until thick, roll as thin as a knife blade and fry in hot lard. Serve with powdered sugar.

FRENCH ROLLS OR TWIST.—1 qt. sweet milk, 1 teaspoon salt, 1 cup good yeast, flour enough to make a stiff batter. When light, add 2 eggs well beaten, 2 teaspoons butter, then knead in flour till stiff enough to roll. Let it raise until quite light, roll, cut in strips and braid it. Bake 30 minutes in buttered tins.

SALLY LUNN.—½ cup of butter warmed in a pint of sweet milk with a little salt, 3 well beaten eggs, 7 cups of sifted flour, ½ cup of yeast. Pour in pans and bake when light.

PUFF MUFFINS.—4 cups milk, 4 cups flour, butter the size of a walnut, 5 eggs, bake ½ hour. For company, 5 cups milk.

POTATO ROLLS.—1 cup very soft mashed potatoes and 1 large tablespoon flour beaten together thoroughly, 2 eggs, ¾ cup sugar, and 1 do. yeast, let it raise, knead them light, adding ½ cup melted butter. Stiffen and knead the same as rusk, let it raise again, roll out and cut, let it raise again.

MADISON ROLLS.—2 medium sized potatoes, mash in the water in which they are boiled to make a pint, 1 egg, lard the size of an egg, 1 cup potato yeast, 1 tablespoon sugar, 1 teaspoon salt. Knead stiff and long.

MUSH CAKES.—Take 1 qt. cold mush, 1 cup yeast, 2 cups flour, a little salt, work well together, set in a warm place to raise. Bake on a griddle. Serve hot.

GRAHAM BREAD.—2 cups sweet milk, 2 do. sour or buttermilk, ½ cup molasses, 1 teaspoon soda, with unbolted wheat meal to make a stiff batter.

WATER CRACKERS.—Mix in 2 quarts flour, 1 cup butter, 3 teaspoons cream tartar, salt, 1½ teaspoons soda, well incorporated, then add 1 pt. water, beat with the rolling pin, cut and prick and bake on a tin or oven bottom with a slow fire.

WIGGS.—Put ½ pt. warm milk to ¾ lbs. of flour, mix in it 2 spoonfuls of light yeast, cover it up and set it before the fire an hour in order to raise, work into it 4 ounces each of sugar and butter, make it into cakes with as little flour as possible. Bake quickly.

CORN MUFFINS.

1. To 1 qt. of meal, ½ cup of lard, 3 eggs, 1 teaspoon soda, scald the meal with water, at the same time add the lard and a little salt, thin with milk, adding the eggs and soda.

2. 2 cups corn meal, 1 cup flour, ⅓ cup sugar, ⅓ do. shortening, 2 eggs, 1 pt. sweet milk, a little salt, 3 teaspoons baking powder.

MEATS.

BEEF STEAK.—Pound well your meat until the fibres break; be sure that next you have to broil the steak, good coals in plenty; nor it a moment leave, but turn it over this way and then that; the lean should be quite rare; not so the fat; the platter now and then the juice receive. Put on your butter, place in your meat, salt, pepper, turn it over, serve and eat.

HAM TOAST.—Scrape or pound some cold ham, mix it with beaten eggs, season well with pepper, lay it on buttered toast, place in a hot oven for three or four minutes.

TO PRESERVE SAUSAGE.—½ gallon water, 1 lb. sugar, 1 pt. salt, let it boil, skim off, let it get cold, then pour over sausages. Sausage put up in this way, covered with this brine, will keep a long time without getting strong.

VEAL CUTLETS.—Have a steak of veal, pound and season well, take 1 egg and beat a little. Dip the steak into the egg and cover well with bread crumbs. Have ready a hot skillet with lard and butter. When nicely browned on both sides, make a gravy of milk, flour and salt.

MINCE MEAT BALLS.—Mince the meat to be used (either fresh or cold, boiled or roasted), very fine; mix with this 1 or 2 onions chopped fine, and 2 handfuls of light bread crumbs (if very dry, soak in a little warm water), add salt to taste and grated nutmeg. When all are thoroughly mixed, add from one to three eggs, according to the quantity of meat, &c., used. Make into balls or cakes like sausage and fry over a medium hot fire until nicely brown.

MINCED BEEF.—3½ lbs. of lean beef without tendons, before cooking chop it fine, mix with it 6 soda crackers rolled very fine, 3 well beaten eggs, 1½ tablespoons salt, 1 teaspoon or less of ground pepper, 4 tablespoons of cream or milk, butter the size of an egg. Mix all thoroughly, make into a loaf, bake 1½ or 2 hours, basting as other roast beef.

FISH.

FRIED EELS.—Parboil them a few minutes, then have your fat ready and fry them. An improvement is to dip them into an egg and crumbs of bread.

CODFISH BALLS.—Take salt codfish that has been cooked just soft enough to take out the bones. When the bones are all out, take some boiled potatoes, two parts potatoes to one part codfish, and add eggs, milk and flour so as to stick well together. Then make them into round balls the size of a small teacup. Bake in hot lard to a nice brown; serve hot. This is a good dish for breakfast.

FRIED FISH.—Have your fish ready cleaned and dry of water, then roll them in corn meal, fry some slices of salt pork, when fried enough take out the pork and put in your fish. Fry slowly to a nice brown, and then they are ready for the table.

SCOLLOPED OYSTERS.—Put a layer of bread crumbs in your dish, then a layer of nice oysters, season with pepper, salt and butter, another layer bread crumbs and oysters, finishing the top with bread crumbs. Pour the liquor over all, and bake.

SOUPS.

BEEF SOUP.—Put on a shin of beef to boil 1 hour before dinner, put in the vegetables — chopped-up potatoes, turnips, tomatoes, or any others you wish; pepper, salt, celery, parsley, or ketchup, 1 egg rolled in flour, stirred in a few minutes before taking out.

TOMATO SOUP.—Take 6 large tomatoes, pare and slice them, drop in 1 pt. boiling water, and let them boil 10 minutes. Add ½ teaspoon soda, 1 qt. sweet milk, three rolled crackers, with butter, pepper and salt to suit the taste. Serve hot, and eat with crackers.

POTATO SOUP.—Take 6 potatoes, pare and grate on a grater, add 2 eggs, and mix well together; cook with about 1 lb. of fat boiling beef in four quarts of water. This is a very good and cheap soup.

VEGETABLE SOUP.—Peel and slice a quart bowl of potatoes with 2 or 3 onions, and boil tender; stir 3 tablespoons of flour into cold water, and add to the potatoes, with butter the size of an egg; pour in water sufficient for 4 quarts of soup, and season with pepper and salt to the taste. Add a pint of dry bread or biscuit, boil a few moments, and serve.

SAUCES.

LEMON SAUCE.—1 cup white sugar, $\frac{1}{2}$ rind of lemon, 1 teaspoon lemon juice, a lump of butter the size of an egg, $\frac{1}{2}$ pt. water, add 1 teaspoon corn starch mixed with a little water; let simmer, but not boil.

FOAM SAUCE.—1 cup sugar, beaten light, 3 tablespoons cold water, put over a kettle of boiling water and stir all the time until cooked; put a piece of butter in a dish, and turn it out; flavor to taste.

CHILI SAUCE.—This is an excellent relish with cold meats. 18 ripe tomatoes, 3 or 4 onions and 3 green peppers chopped fine, 1 cup sugar, $2\frac{1}{2}$ cups vinegar, 2 teaspoons salt, 1 teaspoon each of all kinds of spices. Bottle for use.

KETCHUPS.

CUCUMBER KETCHUPS.

1. 3 doz. full-grown cucumbers, split and take out the large seeds, cut on the slaw cutter, 4 white onions sliced, $1\frac{1}{2}$ cups fine salt; mix and drain over night, then mix with them $\frac{1}{2}$ cup black pepper, 1 do. black mustard seed; boil the vinegar, and pour over when cold; cover the vessel with white cloths, and put on top of it pieces of dishes to serve as weight.

2. 6 qts. grated cucumbers, 1 qt. onions chopped fine, $\frac{1}{2}$ cup white mustard seed to the same quantity of black mustard seed, a cayenne pepper, 2 tablespoons table oil, 2 spoons black pepper, grate the cucumbers, then add $\frac{3}{4}$ cup salt; drain over night, then add all the ingredients, covering with good vinegar. Bottle, and it is ready for use.

3. 3 doz. full-grown cucumbers, 6 or 8 onions, pare and slice them, sprinkle with $\frac{1}{2}$ pt. fine salt; lay them in a colander to drain 5 or 6 hours, then measure them. This ought to yield 5 qts. Put in 1 cup of mustard seed and $\frac{1}{2}$ cup black pepper, 6 doz. cloves, a little mace, mix well together, put in a jar, cover with vinegar, tie up closely.

TOMATO KETCHUP.

1. 1 pk. tomatoes, 1 oz. cinnamon, 1 oz. cloves, $\frac{3}{4}$ pt. sugar, 1 tablespoon salt, 1 teaspoon cayenne pepper, 1 pt. good vinegar. Boil tomatoes, cinnamon, cloves, sugar, and salt one hour and a half. When nearly done, add vinegar and pepper. Before adding cinnamon and cloves, tie in a piece of muslin.

2. 1 pk. of tomatoes, and boil them soft and rub them through a wire sieve, then add 1 pt. vinegar, 2 tablespoons salt, 1 oz. allspice, ½ oz. cloves, 1 tablespoon black pepper, mix and boil 3 hours, or until it is reduced one-half. Bottle when cold.

3. Take ripe tomatoes, boil well, put through the colander, to 2 qts. add 2 oz. cloves, 1 oz. black pepper, 1 nutmeg, a little cayenne pepper, salt to taste, nearly 1 pt. cider vinegar, and a small cup sugar. Boil well.

4. Chop fine 1½ pks. ripe tomatoes, grate 2 roots of horse-radish, 1 cup onions cut fine, 1 do. salt, 1 do. black pepper, 2 red peppers, cut fine, 3 or 4 stalks of celery, cut fine, 1 tablespoonful of powdered cloves, 1 do. mace, 1 do. cinnamon, 1 do. celery seed, 1½ cups sugar, 1 qt. vinegar. Put the celery seed in vinegar, and just let them come to the boil together; when cold, pour on the ingredients, cut your tomatoes and put in the colander to drain. While you prepare the other things, use the juice of your onions, too. If celery is out of the question, finely-cut cabbage will do, but not nearly so good, with more celery seed. Seal it up, and it will keep till next spring.

PICKLES.

PICKLE LILY.

1. Chop 1 pk. green tomatoes, stir in 1 teacup salt, strain in a colander over night, add to it 6 green peppers, chopped fine, 1 teacup grated horse-radish, 2 qts. vinegar, 1 teacup sugar. Let it boil gently, stirring it occasionally until the tomatoes are cooked, then adding cloves, nutmeg, 1 teaspoon of each.

2. 1 pk. green tomatoes, 1 doz. onions, slice the tomatoes and salt them thoroughly, put in a bag to drain for 12 hours; do the same with the onions. Spice with whole cloves, ginger root, allspice, mace and mustard seed. Cover with good cider vinegar, and boil all together for one hour.

PICKLED PEACHES.

1. ½ pt. vinegar, ½ pt. water, 3 lbs. white sugar. Let the syrup come to a boil, then divide ½ pk. peaches into 3 parts, letting each part boil 20 minutes, making 60 minutes for the syrup; add cloves and cinnamon. If the syrup becomes too thick, add a little water.

2. Take nice large peaches, not too ripe, wipe off the fur or down with a soft flannel cloth, place three or four cloves in each one, and lay them whole in a jar. To every gal. vinegar, add 1 qt. water, 5 lbs. sugar, 1 tablespoon salt, and whole cinnamon. Pour it over the fruit boiling hot, being careful that the vinegar covers them well. Let them stand in a cool place for a few days, then turn the liquor off and boil again.

3. Take peaches, pretty ripe, but not mellow, wipe with a flannel cloth as smooth as possible. Stick a few cloves in each peach, 1 lb. sugar, 1 pt. vinegar. Boil the vinegar, put in your peaches, boil until nearly soft, remove the peaches and boil the vinegar five minutes longer, and pour over the fruit. Spice with cinnamon, cloves, mace, etc.

4. 1 pk. of cling peaches (white), 3 lbs. white sugar, 1 pt. cider vinegar. Pour boiling water over the peaches, and rub them with a dry cloth, and drop them in cold water. Then put them in boiling water and let them boil until you can run a straw into them; then take out of the water and put them into the vinegar and sugar and let them boil fifteen minutes. Can hot in glass or stone jars.

5. Take ripe peaches, rub off the fur, take equal portions of vinegar and sugar, sufficient to cover, and a few cloves. Bring to boil; pour on hot. For sour pickles, omit the sugar.

CUCUMBER PICKLES.

1. Put the cucumbers for three days in salt water, closely covered. For 200 small cucumbers, take 3 tablespoons white mustard seed, 3 do. black mustard seed, 3 do. celery seed, 1 handful juniper berries, 1 handful small green peppers, and 2 lbs. sugar. Add some small onions, and boil fifteen minutes in ½ gal. vinegar. Add to this 1 jar of English chow-chow and a little alum. Pour the whole scalding hot over the pickles; pour the vinegar back into the kettle 3 or 4 times, each time pouring it boiling hot over the cucumbers; then when ready to bottle, mix ½ lb. ground mustard with some cold vinegar, and also the vinegar from off the chow-chow, and fill into glass jars. Seal up tight. Not ready to use for six weeks.

2. Take 1 doz. large ripe cucumbers, pare and slice ½ inch thick, 1 lb. white sugar, 1 qt. vinegar, ½ oz. whole cloves, ½ oz. stick cinnamon; put the spices into a bag, and place all in a porcelain-lined kettle and boil slowly until the cucumbers are soft. Put into stone jars and set away for use. Mushmelons are pickled in the same way.

3. Pack in jars and cover with good cider vinegar, let stand three or four weeks, then drain off and put on fresh vinegar, cover over closely with horse-radish leaves. Pickles put up in this way will keep a long time. The cucumbers should be put into the vinegar without being salted.

SPANISH PICKLE.—2 doz. well grown cucumbers, ½ pk. green tomatoes, ½ doz. green peppers, 1 doz. large onions, sliced; cut the cucumbers in slices about an inch thick, without peeling, slice the tomatoes, cut the beans in two, sprinkle with salt, and let stand twenty-four hours, then wash off the salt; take some horse-radish, 1 lb. white mustard seed, a few red peppers, chopped, 3 oz. cinnamon; make a paste of 1 lb. flour of mustard, 2 oz. tumeric, and a bottle of sweet oil; mix in 2 or 3 oz. (according to taste) of celery seed. Put your vegetables into a large pan, and mix the spices and paste all through them, then scald enough good vinegar to cover them; put the vegetables into a jar, pour the boiling water over them, having added brown sugar to taste. Every few days stir it well, and in two weeks it will be ready for use.

FLINT PICKLES (CUCUMBERS).—Make a brine of a teacup of salt to a gallon of water, which is to be heated for ten mornings and poured over your pickles; on morning of tenth day in clear water, and let them stand for three or four hours, after which dry them off with a cloth; put them in enough strong cider vinegar to cover them, heating the vinegar when pickles are in it, just permitting it to come to a boil, putting whole cloves, allspice, pepper, horse-radish and onions in if you desire.

CANTALOUPE PICKLES.

1. Ripe cantaloupes, pare and take out the pulp, cover with vinegar, and let them stand twenty-four hours, then add 3 lbs. sugar, cinnamon, cloves, and allspice; boil all fifteen minutes; put in the fruit, boil fifteen or twenty minutes; take out the fruit, and boil the syrup fifteen or twenty minutes. Put them in a jar, pour the syrup over the fruit and then it is fit for use.

2. Pare and slice the fruit, and let it stand over night in weak vinegar; then, to 7 lbs. fruit make a syrup of 1 qt. vinegar, 3 lbs. sugar, $\frac{1}{4}$ oz. cloves, $\frac{1}{2}$ oz. whole mace, 1 oz. cinnamon. Put the fruit into the syrup and let it cook until you can run a straw through the fruit.

GREEN TOMATO PICKLES.

1. Peel the tomatoes, slice them thin, pour boiling water over them, and let stand over night; take 3 pts. vinegar, and 2 lbs. sugar to 12 lbs. fruit, spice to taste; scald the vinegar and spices, and pour over three times; the last time scald the fruit with the vinegar.

2. $\frac{1}{2}$ pk. green tomatoes sliced on the slaw knife, 6 or 8 onions sliced as above, salt, and let them drain two hours; $\frac{1}{2}$ cup white mustard, 1 teaspoon black pepper, ground, 1 teaspoon black mustard, 1 lb. sugar, 1 pt. vinegar—the latter together, and put over; the same quantity the three following mornings so as to cover.

3. Slice green tomatoes into a vessel, salt slightly, pour on boiling water, let stand over night; next morning drain off the water, put in a vessel a layer of tomatoes, and if liked, a layer of onions alternately, take vinegar sufficient to cover, and throw in of all the different spices; bring the vinegar to a boil, and pour over the pickles. In a few days they are ready for use.

4. 1 pk. green tomatoes, 3 doz. small onions, sliced and salted twenty-four hours; 1 box mustard, $\frac{1}{4}$ lb. mustard seed, 1 oz. black pepper, 1 oz. cloves, and 1 oz. allspice; drain all the water off the tomatoes; boil in a small kettle three hours; sufficient vinegar to cover them; add a cup of sugar, and a small teaspoon of red pepper. Put in small stone jars.

5. 1 gallon of finely sliced tomatoes, 1 gallon of cut cabbage, 2 doz. of very small cucumbers, left whole, and half a doz. green peppers, sliced; boil the tomatoes and cabbage a few minutes in salt water; while draining take 1 gal. of vinegar, 1 lb. sugar, 1 oz. allspice, 1 oz. cloves, 1 oz. cinnamon, 1 oz. tumeric, $\frac{1}{4}$ lb. mustard seed, $\frac{1}{2}$ oz. pepper, 1 oz. celery seed—boil together a few minutes, and throw it over the tomatoes, cabbage, cucumbers and peppers.

6. To 1 qt. vinegar take 1 lb. sugar—cloves, cinnamon and mustard to taste; slice the tomatoes, put in a crock over night with a little salt, in the morning drain off the salt; put in a kettle with 1 qt. good cider vinegar, and cook till a little soft, skim out the tomatoes and put in the spice, boil with a little horse-radish cut in bits; pour over the tomatoes; let stand ten days or two weeks, pour off the juice and boil it, put over again and let stand two weeks, boil juice again; if it then needs sugar, add some.

TOMATO CHOWDER.—Soak a peck green tomatoes 24 hours in salt water, chop them fine, adding 3 onions, mix with them 1 teacup white mustard seed, scald them with vinegar sufficient to cover them. Spicing with pepper, cloves, allspice, tied in a bag. Cover tight.

TOMATO HIGDON.—Grind the tomatoes in a sausage grinder, cover them with vinegar and let stand over night, then strain twice through a cloth, chop onions, (to your taste,) celery, pepper crushed, (not ground,) cloves crushed, cinnamon crushed, cauliflower cut fine, and mustard seed. Boil good cider vinegar and throw over it after mixing it thoroughly. Keep it well covered with the vinegar.

MELON MANGOES.—Mangoes, 50; cucumbers, 50. Put in salt water eight days; they can be in for weeks or months, but will have to stand in a mixture of $\frac{1}{3}$ water and $\frac{2}{3}$ vinegar to draw salt out, make a stuffing of 2 heads of cabbage, cut fine with salt sprinkled on it, 1 doz. onions, $\frac{1}{2}$ pt. nasturtiums, 1 lb. mustard seed, 1 oz. cloves, 1 oz. allspice, $\frac{1}{2}$ oz. mace, 6 or 8 nutmegs, $\frac{1}{4}$ oz. turmeric, 3 red peppers, 1 small teaspoon cayenne pepper, and stuff with the mixture. Horse-radish grated or cut in pieces; $\frac{1}{4}$ pt. whisky, $\frac{1}{2}$ cup sugar. Oil should be put on all pickles.

PICKLED CHERRIES.—1 qt. seeded cherries, 1 lb. sugar, 1$\frac{1}{2}$ pts. vinegar, boil the sugar and vinegar together *5 times*, let stand over night. Each time throw it over the cherries while boiling.

PICKLED BLACKBERRIES.—3 qts. blackberries, 1 qt. vinegar, 1 qt. sugar. No spice is required. Put all together at the same time into your kettle and boil 10 or 15 minutes. After standing a few weeks, they are very nice.

WALNUT PICKLES.—Take green walnuts when yet tender enough to run a pin through, put them in salt pickle for 10 days, then let simmer in fresh water until heated through, then spread on plates in a dry cool place, and leave them until they turn black, then put in jars, a layer of walnuts, then a layer of spices until full, then cover with good cold vinegar. Use cloves, mustard, ginger, allspice, pepper, or any spice to taste.

YELLOW PICKLE.—3 gals. pure cider vinegar, ½ lb. coriander seed, ground, ¼ lb. Jamaica ginger, ground, 1 doz. lemons cut in rings, 3 oz. ground cloves, 3 oz. ground allspice, 3 oz. turmeric, ¼ lb. each of yellow and brown mustard seed, whole; ½ lb. horse-radish cut in strips, 1 qt. little onions, 3 oz. whole mace, 3 oz. whole celery seed, 2 lbs. brown sugar, 1 teacup salt. Put the vinegar in a stone jar covered securely and set out in the sun in August, put in the vinegar, your spices, seeds, and lemon. The horse-radish, sugar and salt, you put in the fall, when you put your pickles, &c., in. The onions before putting in must be slightly scalded and peeled. We put in the following: Small pickles the size of your finger, gather when you can and pack in salt, then in the fall when ready to put in the vinegar, stuffed peppers, radish pods, beans, quite small ears of corn, scalded; cauliflower and quite small heads of cabbage, scalded and cut in pieces; put in anything that is good when pickled. Put pickles and vegetables in at one time in the fall, or whenever you have them all ready. If they don't get as yellow as you like, add a little more turmeric.

To preserve pickles from white specks, add a little horse-radish.

CORN, VEGETABLES, ETC.

CANNED CORN.

1. 1¼ oz. tartaric acid dissolved in ½ pt. water, measure your corn, put in kettle, corn with water, and bring to the boil, then to 1 pt. corn add 1 tablespoon of the acid solution. Put in cans. An hour before using a can, open and put in 1 teaspoon soda to 1 qt. corn.

2. To 1 qt. corn, take 1 small teaspoon tartaric acid, put the acid into the kettle with a small quantity of water, then the corn, and cook thoroughly, stirring constantly. It must be quite tart with the acid. Seal tightly. When opened for use, cook but very little and add a small teaspoon soda to neutralize the acid; too much soda makes the corn yellow.

CORN OYSTERS.

1. Six large ears of corn (grated), 1 cup sweet cream, 2 teaspoons flour, 3 eggs, yolks and whites beaten separately, stir the whites in after all the other parts are mixed. Season with pepper and salt.

2. 1 qt. green corn rasped on a coarse grater, 2 cups new milk, 1 cup flour, mix together and add 2 eggs, well beaten. Season the batter with pepper and salt, and bake on a griddle.

3. 2 doz. ears of corn, grated, 5 eggs, 3 tablespoons flour, season to taste, and fry in butter.

4. Mix 1 pt. of grated sweet corn with 3 tablespoons milk, 1 teacup flour, 1 large teaspoon melted butter, 1 teaspoon salt, 1 small pepper and 1 egg; drop this mixture by the large spoon into your frying pan, and fry them until brown; use butter for frying. These are nice served up with meat for dinner.

5. 1½ doz. ears of corn grated, 3 large tablespoons sifted flour, the yolks of 6 eggs well beaten; fry in butter.

6. 1 pt. grated corn, raw, 1 cup flour, 2 eggs, salt and pepper; fry in lard.

SWEET POTATOES MADE OF IRISH POTATOES.—2 qts. mashed potatoes, 1 cup sugar, and 2 eggs. If too stiff when mixed, add ½ cup sweet cream, then put your flour on your moulding board and mould them into the shape of sweet potatoes, lay them in a pan, and put them in the oven to brown.

COOKED POTATOES.—2 doz. potatoes, peel and cut fine, wash and cook in salt water. When cooked, add ½ pt. sour cream and 1 tablespoon flour.

POTATO CAKES.—Have ready some boiled potatoes, mashed, 1 qt. sweet milk, 2 eggs, flour enough to make a thick batter. Bake in hot fat.

SARATOGA POTATOES.—Peel and slice, let stand over night in salt water, drain next morning and put in boiling fat, let come to a chestnut brown, take out, drain, and dish up.

BAKED BEANS.—Take white soup beans, as many as you wish for one meal, boil them until soft, just so as not to burst, then strain them through a colander. When a little cool, put them in earthen jars holding 2 quarts, fill up your jars with the beans, but not too full, then put in 1 tablespoon molasses, ½ tablespoon mustard, then have some salt pork sliced in thin pieces, then put in slices of pork over the beans in the jars, then fill up the jars with water to the top, and keep water on them while baking, so as to prevent them from burning; put them in a cooking-stove oven, and bake ½ day — that time being required to bake them right. After being prepared in this way they are considered most wholesome.

CAULIFLOWER.—Salt 1 day, in the evening press out so that no juice remains, let the vinegar come to a boil, mix the mustard to a paste, stir it when boiling, then put the cabbage in and stir till heated through.

STUFFED CABBAGE.—Hash together equal parts of meat and potatoes, season well with pepper and salt; hollow out a head of cabbage, and fill in the meat and potatoes, tie together, and boil one hour.

SMOTHERED TOMATOES.—Take any number of smooth, ripe tomatoes, wash and dry well, place in a stew pan, sprinkle flour over them, add a lump of butter the size of an egg, salt and pepper to taste; cover close with a lid, and allow them to stew about 15 minutes, then turn and stew the same length of time.

FRIED TOMATOES.—The vegetables should not be too ripe. Cut in slices about ½ inch thick; have prepared a dish of flour, with pepper and salt to taste, then roll the slices separately in the flour, and fry in hot lard or butter.

SCALLOPED TOMATOES.—First cut and peel the tomatoes. A layer of bread crumbs, then a layer of tomatoes alternately till the pan is full, with pepper, salt, a little sugar and butter; have the crumbs last, over which spread 1 beaten egg; bake ¾ of an hour.

SALADS, ETC.

CHICKEN SALADS.

1. 1 chicken steamed and cut in strips, twice as much cabbage or celery as chicken, 3 eggs boiled and mashed, with 1 tablespoon butter, while hot; season well with pepper and salt, and add vinegar enough to make it moist.

2. 1 chicken, 3 yolks of hard-boiled eggs, 4 tablespoons oil, 1 teaspoon salt, red pepper, tablespoon vinegar, 1 tablespoon mustard, 2 large bunches of celery.

COLD SLAW.—Shave a head white cabbage very fine; for 1 qt. of this slaw take yolks of 3 eggs, beaten well, stir into them 1½ tumblers good vinegar, 2 teaspoons loaf sugar, 1 tablespoon thick sweet cream (and a tablespoon olive oil if preferred), butter the size of a walnut, 1 tablespoon mixed mustard, salt and pepper to taste; mix all together with the yolks, and put into a stew pan. When boiling hot, add the cabbage; stew only four or five minutes; toss it frequently from the bottom with a silver or wooden fork; dish the slaw, and put it where it will become perfectly cold—on ice, if possible. If the vinegar is very strong, use less in proportion.

DRESSING FOR COLD SLAW.—Beat well the yolk of an egg, add a little milk, 2 or 3 tablespoons vinegar, and a small piece of butter, bringing all to a boil, stirring all the time; pour over the slaw *hot*. It is delicious.

TURNIP SLAW.—Cut turnips the size of a bean, add ½ cup lard, pepper and salt, boil them soft; beat an egg with a tablespoon of flour and vinegar, and pour over.

CANNED FRUIT.

CANNED PEACHES.—12 lbs. peaches, 4 lbs. sugar, 1 pt. best cider vinegar, wash the peaches in warm water, rub with a dry cloth, put in the syrup and boil until tender. Can whole, and fill the jar to the top with syrup.

CANNED GRAPES.—Place the grapes in an earthen vessel. Let it stand in the stove and pour upon the grapes boiling water. After steaming a few minutes, dip them out with a wire egg beater, into cans, and fill up the cans with a syrup of sugar boiled in water, using only water enough to dissolve the sugar. Apply it boiling hot.

For Canning Strawberries.—At the commencement of the strawberry season, make 2 or 3 qts. of white sugar into a thick syrup by dissolving it in hot water, 2 large coffee cups to a qt. Boil and skim this and put into jug or bottles for future use. Put your ripe, fresh strawberries into glass cans, and fill up with cold syrup nearly to the brim, as the strawberries shrink somewhat. Place in a kettle of cold water, putting the lids on the top of the cans first, but not screwing them down. Let them come to a boil slowly; boil for five minutes, then screw the lids down tightly, and set away in a dark place.

PRESERVES, FRUITS, JELLIES, ETC.

Dried Apple Jelly.—Take 6 lbs. dried apples, cover them with water and let them soak over night. Next morning let them cook a short time, strain through a jelly-bag, add 1 tincup sugar to 1 tincup juice. Flavor with 2 lemons.

Pine Apple Jam.—Take 10 lbs. grated pine apple, 6 lbs. sugar, and boil 1 hour.

Quince Marmalade.—Take quinces that are quite ripe, pare and cut in quarters, take out the cores, put them in a stew pan with spring water, nearly enough to cover them, keep them covered and let them stew gently until they are quite soft and red, then mash and rub through a wire sieve. Put in a pan over a gentle fire with as much thick clarified sugar as the weight of the quinces; boil them an hour and stir the whole time with a wooden spoon to prevent sticking. Put into pots, and when cold tie them up.

To Preserve Damsons.—Boil 3 lbs. sugar with 6 lbs. damsons over a slow fire till the juice adheres to the fruit and forms a jam.

Apple Jelly.—Take of apple juice 4 lbs., strained; sugar 1 lb., and boil it to a jelly. Raspberry juice 4 lbs., 2 lbs. sugar, and boil down.

Gooseberry Jelly.—Dissolve sugar in about half its weight of water, and boil. It will be nearly solid when cold. To this syrup add an equal weight of gooseberries.

Blackberry Preserves.—1 pt. currant juice, 6 lbs. blackberries, give them their weight in sugar, and boil till the syrup is rich.

Preserved Peaches for Pies.—15 lbs. peaches, 5 lbs. sugar. Boil five hours, add 1½ pts. vinegar, boil 15 minutes, then can and seal.

Strawberry Jelly.—Squeeze out the juice of the strawberries, and to each pt. of juice add ¾ lb. lump sugar, boil for twenty minutes, turn into cups which have been previously dipped in cold water, and set in the sun for a few hours.

DRINKS.

CHERRY VINEGAR.—To 6 qts. sour cherries (not seeded) add 1 qt. good vinegar. Mash well and stand away for three days, then strain and to each pt. of juice add ½ pt. sugar. Boil ½ hour, then it is ready to drink. It can be bottled and kept for years if desired.

CURRANT WINE.—1 qt. juice of currants, 2 qts. water, 3 lbs. damp brown sugar, ferment in tubs, skim every day until done working, then put it in a keg; put the bung in loose until done working, then drive tight.

PATENT GAS SHERBET—*The best and healthiest drink in use.*—Put 1½ lbs. white sugar into a crock, pour on it 1 pt. hot water. Add 1 oz. baking soda; mix it well. Then beat the whites of 2 eggs well; mix ½ tablespoon flour into the eggs, beat it well and mix all together, then flavor with ½ teaspoon lemon oil, or any other flavor you wish. Then mix separately ½ oz. tartaric acid with ½ pt. cold water. This makes enough for 125 glasses of drink.

FOR MAKING BEER.—To 9 qts. water (heated) take 1½ lbs. brown sugar, 1½ pts. good fresh yeast, 1½ tablespoons ginger, *1 cent's worth* whole cloves, 1 teaspoon cream tartar, let stand 1½ days, then strain and bottle up tight.

SUGAR BEER.—Take 2½ lbs. white sugar, 1 large tablespoon ginger, ½ do. cream tartar, 1 teaspoon cinnamon, 1 grated nutmeg, and 1 pt. good hop yeast. Put into a tin bucket and mix well; then add 3 gals. warm water, and pour from one vessel into another until it is thoroughly mixed; tie a cloth over the top and set in the sun. Let it stand over night, and strain carefully, bottle, cork and wire next morning, and set in the sun a few hours, after which put it in a cool place for two or three days, when it will be ready for use.

GINGER POP.

1. 1 lemon cut in slices, 1 tablespoon ginger, as much sugar as will sweeten, throw 1 gal. boiling water on it, and let stand until cold; then add 1 cup yeast. Let stand over night and it will be ready for use.

2. 2 gallons water, 2 lbs. white sugar, 2 oz. ginger root, 1½ cups fresh yeast, 1½ oz. cream tartar. Put the ginger in the two gallons of cold water, then put it on the stove and let boil twenty minutes; then put in the sugar and let cool pretty well, then put in the cream tartar and yeast. Let stand 24 hours, strain it, and bottle for use.

RASPBERRY VINEGAR.—To 2 qts. raspberries, slightly bruised, add 1 qt. of good vinegar, and let stand over night; strain through a flannel bag, and to 1 pt. of juice add 1 pt. sugar, and heat until the sugar dissolves. Bottle and cork for use.

RASPBERRY CORDIAL.—To 1 gal. fruit, take 1 qt. strong vinegar; pour over and let stand 24 hours, and strain; boil fifteen minutes. To one pt. of syrup add 1 lb. sugar.

BLACKBERRY SYRUP.—It is said to be almost a specific cure for summer complaint, and in 1832 was used with success in the cholera. To 2 quarts blackberry juice, add the following ingredients: 1 lb. loaf sugar, $\frac{1}{2}$ oz. nutmeg, $\frac{1}{4}$ oz. cinnamon, $\frac{1}{4}$ oz. cloves, $\frac{1}{4}$ oz. allspice. Boil together for a short time, and when cold add 1 pt. brandy, or 1 gill 98 per cent. alcohol and 1 gill of water. From a teaspoon to a wine glass, according to the age of the patient, is to be given at proper intervals, until relieved.

BLACKBERRY SHRUP.—5 qts. berries, mash them well, then pour 1 qt. vinegar over them, strain it, and to every pt. of juice add 1 lb. white sugar. Boil to a thin syrup, bottle and cork tight.

ELDERBERRY WINE.—1 qt. of juice, 3 qts. of water, 3 lbs. of white sugar. Put in a large crock and set in the cellar, skimming every morning for a week; then strain and bottle, and as it ferments off, keep filling up.

CREAM TARTAR BEER.—8 qts. water to 1 qt. molasses, 2 tablespoons cream tartar, 1 do. ginger, or more, 1 do. allspice, $\frac{1}{2}$ pt. yeast. Let stand over night, shire off, let stand $\frac{1}{2}$ hour, then bottle.

BLACKBERRY WINE.

1. 4 qts. juice, 2 qts. water, 4 lbs. sugar; set in the cellar, same as elderberry.

2. Mash the berries, and pour 1 pt. boiling water to each gal. Let the mixture stand 12 hours, stirring occasionally; then strain and measure into a keg, adding 2 lbs. sugar and 1 qt. good rye whisky, or 1 pt. best alcohol to each gal. Cork tight and let stand two or three months. Use a clean keg, and then you will have the wine ready for use.

LEMON SYRUP.—Squeeze the juice of 25 lemons, strain it and add 1 pt. water, 2 lbs. sugar; let it simmer. Bottle it.

GINGER BEER.—1 gal. cold water, 1 lb. white sugar, $\frac{1}{2}$ oz. race ginger, 1 sliced lemon, 1 teacup yeast. Let it stand all night to ferment, then pour it off with stirring, bottle it, and add 1 raisin to each bottle.

BEER.—$\frac{1}{4}$ lb. ginger, 1 cent's worth of cloves, 1 oz. cream tartar, scald these and add 1 pt. hop yeast to 3 gallons water, and sweeten to taste.

TO MAKE BEER.—1 pt. molasses, 1 pt. yeast, 6 pints water, 1 tablespoon allspice and cinnamon.

MISCELLANEOUS.

HOW TO MAKE SOAP.—Slack 5 lbs. lime with hot water, then add $6\frac{1}{2}$ lbs. soda ash to it, and pour $4\frac{1}{2}$ large buckets of boiling water on it; then stir well, let stand over night; then pour the clear lye to 15 lbs. rendered fat, or 25 lbs. bacon skins, into a kettle. Then pour 4 buckets boiling water on the soda ash, and lime again to make your lye. Now boil your fat 1 hour, then add $1\frac{1}{2}$ pts. salt, boil 1 hour longer; then put the soap into a tub, let stand over night, replace it in the kettle again and pour the 4 buckets of weak lye to it. Boil 2 hours, then add $1\frac{1}{2}$ pts. more salt. Boil half an hour.

HARD SOAP.—To 6 lbs. soap-fat, take 6 lbs. soda, and 3 lbs. lime. Boil the soda and lime in 4 gals. of water, pour off the clear liquor, taking care to get no sediment. Add this to your fat, boil until soap, pour it out, and when cold, cut as desired. This needs no salting.

SOAP.—6 lbs. good lime, 6 lbs. soda ash, 12 lbs. rendered fat, 15 gals. water. Put the lime and soda ash in the kettle with all the water, and let it boil from 5 to 10 minutes smartly. Then put in a tub to settle, which it will do in a few minutes. Dip it back into the kettle and add the fat. Boil 4 or 5 hours. No salt, or it will be ruined.

ERASIVE SOAP.—2 oz. aqua ammonia, 1 oz. white shaving soap, 1 teaspoon saltpetre, 1 qt. soft water.

The sender of the above recipe says it is worth ten dollars to any family, and costs but little to try it.

FOR REMOVING GREASE, ETC.—2 oz. castile soap, 2 oz. strongest ammonia, $\frac{1}{2}$ oz. ether, $\frac{1}{2}$ oz. alcohol, cut the soap fine and heat in a pint of soft water until dissolved; then add $\frac{1}{2}$ gal. more water and all the ingredients. Keep corked tight. Cleans all kinds of cloth, carpets, paints, glass, etc., and is a good shampoo for the head. Use sponge, and rinse afterward in clear water. Cost of the above ingredients, 25 cents.

TO REMOVE INK STAINS.—In a teacup of hot water dissolve 1 teaspoon oxalic acid and rub the stained part thoroughly with it.

TO REMOVE STAINS.—Salts of lemon. Put on ink, iron rust or other stains. Pour boiling water over it.

TO TAKE STAINS OUT OF MAHOGANY.—Mix spirits of salts, 6 parts, and salt of lemon, 1 part. Drop a little on the stains, and rub until they disappear.

TO REMOVE MILDEW.—Take 2 oz. chloride of lime, pour on it a qt. of boiling water, then add 3 qts. cold water, steep the linen twelve hours, when every spot will be removed. It will also remove fruit stains. Another way to remove fruit stains, is to pour boiling water through the stains before putting the garment into the wash.

TO DESTROY ANTS.—Simply put a piece of tobacco under each foot of the cupboard. Keep the tobacco moistened a day or two, and your trouble will be over. The above is the only use for tobacco in our house.

SPRIGS of wintergreen will drive away red ants; branches of wormwood will answer the same purpose for black ants.

BED BUG EXTERMINATOR.—To 1 pt. spirits turpentine, add $1\frac{1}{2}$ oz. corrosive sublimate. Let stand 24 hours to extract strength. Then feather the liquid into the cracks and crevices in the room; apply to the furniture, etc. Close the room up tight for two days, or if the room must be used for sleeping, raise the window 6 or 8 inches. I guarantee that if made and used according to directions, it is a dead shot to that household pest—the bed-bug.

To PREVENT moths in carpets, wash the floor before laying them with spirits of turpentine or benzine.

AN EXCELLENT YEAST.—Boil 2 handfuls hops and 3 or 4 potatoes in 2 qts. water, with it scald 3 cups flour. When cold, add 1 cup sugar, 1 tablespoon salt, 1 do. ginger, and 1 cup yeast.

FOR RISING TO KEEP LONG.—12 ordinary sized potatoes, 1 qt. flour, 2 cups sugar, 3 tablespoons even full salt, 5 qts. boiling water, in which the potatoes have been boiled, into that amount. Take 3 yeast cakes, dissolve in 1 pt. cold water, and add to the others when cold.

LIQUID BLUING.—1 oz. oxalic acid (pulverized), 1 oz. Prussian blue (pulverized), mix in 1 qt. soft water, and bottle.

LIQUID BLACKING.—Best ivory black, $\frac{1}{2}$ lb.; treacle, $\frac{1}{4}$ lb.; castor or sweet oil, $\frac{1}{2}$ oz. Mix well together, then add 2 oz. oil of vitriol and enough vinegar to make a quart of liquid.

INDELIBLE INK.—1 inch of stick of nitrate of silver added to any black ink makes it good marking fluid.

To RENEW OLD BLACK LACE.—Rub beeswax on a hot iron and press the lace. Repeat the operation until the lace is stiff enough.

To PATCH OLD CARPET.—Put a patch on neatly with flour paste, and press with a hot iron.

To REMOVE A CANCER WART.—Take horse sorrel, bruise it and strain through a cloth. Set the juice in the sun till it gets like salve. Apply it about an eighth of an inch thick and it will remove the wart in a very short time.

BAKING POWDER.—14 oz. tartaric acid, 16 oz. bi carb. soda, 30 oz. flour. Run through a sieve five or six times so as to mix well.

To PRESERVE BUTTER FOR TWO YEARS.—10 oz. common salt pulverized, 2 oz. best brown sugar, 2 oz. saltpetre. Mix these well. To a pound of butter, add 1 oz. of the mixture; work well, pack close; not fit for use for one month.

POLISH FOR GLASS, SILVER, ETC.—1 lb. whiting, $\frac{1}{2}$ oz. sal. soda. Dissolve the soda in hot water and mix the whiting to a stiff paste.

SUPERIOR CEMENT.—Melt 1 lb. glue without water, or as little water as possible. When melted add 1 lb. rosin and 4 oz. of either red lead, Venetian red or whiting.

FINE CHEAP COLOGNE.—1 qt. 95 per cent. alcohol, 1 oz. oil of lemon, $\frac{1}{2}$ oz. oil of bergamot. Shake thoroughly.

COUGH SYRUP.—1 handful of mullein leaves, 1 handful hoarhound, put 1 qt. water on each in separate vessels, and boil down to a pt., then put together, add 1 pt. best molasses, and boil to a syrup.

VINEGAR.—To make good vinegar, put stripes of slippery elm bark in cider to form mother, and some branches of grape vine to make sharp.

To Clean White Leather Gloves.—White leather gloves may be cleaned to look very nice—putting one on at a time, going over them thoroughly with a shaving brush and lather, then wipe them off with a clean handkerchief or sponge, and dry them on the hands by the fire or in the sun.

To Clean the Inside of a Stove.—Introduce the poker or some other convenient instrument by moving the top of the stove or otherwise, and scrape off the slag while red hot.

Spitting of Blood.—Take 2 spoons juice of nettles at night, or take three spoons sage juice in a little honey. This will presently stop either spitting or vomiting blood; or 20 grains of alum in water every two hours.

Cure for Wrinkles.—First a contented mind, and then to keep the skin soft, a few drops of pure glycerine added to plenty of fresh water early in the morning.

Cure for a Fit of Passion.—Walk out into the open air. You may speak your mind to the winds without hurting anyone, or proclaiming yourself to be a simpleton.

Cocoanut Candy Quickly Made.—Grate the meat of a cocoanut, and having ready 2 lbs. finely sifted white sugar, the beaten whites of 2 eggs, and the milk of the nut, simply mix all together and make little cakes. In a short time the candy will be dry enough to use.

German Toast.—Cut bread in slices, dip them first in sweet milk, then in beaten eggs; have a pan hot, with just sufficient butter to fry. Serve with sugar.

Breakfast Dish.—Slice some light bread, fry slightly in butter or gravy, beat 3 or 4 eggs with $\frac{1}{2}$ cup new milk, and a little salt; when the bread is hot, pour the eggs over it, cover for a few minutes, stir lightly, so that the eggs may be cooked.

French Toast.—Beat 4 eggs very light, and stir with them 1 pt. of milk, slice bread, dip pieces into the egg, fry in hot lard till a nice brown; sprinkle sugar and cinnamon on each, and serve hot. Light bread will be equal to waffles.

How to Take Out Rust.—1 oz. oxalic acid in $\frac{1}{2}$ pt. water. Wash your clothes, put this on them, lay in the sun for ten minutes, wash again and boil.

Peach Leather.—Stew peaches as if for pies, take out the stones and make into a pulp, put this on plain boards on a roof, in the sun. In a few days it will be dry enough to peel off the boards, roll it and put it away dry.

Chocolate Cream Drops.—$\frac{1}{2}$ cup of cream, 2 cups white sugar, boil 5 minutes, set the dish in another one of cold water, stir until it gets hard, then make in small balls; with a fork roll each in the chocolate ($\frac{3}{4}$ cake) which has in the meantime been put in a pan over boiling water and melted. Put them on paper to cool.

CURE FOR A SNAKE BITE.—Take poke root and boil it, hold the bite over it and steam it while it is boiling, then bathe it in the same water. If not poke root, take salt water.

A RECIPE FOR MAKING TATTLERS.—Take a handful of the weed called Run-about, the same amount of root called Nimble-Tongue, a sprig of the herb called Backbite, either before or after dog-days, a tablespoon of Don't-you-tell-it, 6 drachms of Malice, a few drops of Envy, which can be purchased at the shops of Miss Tabitha Tea-table and Miss Nancy Night-walker. Stir all well together, and simmer half an hour over the fire of Discontent, kindled with a little Jealousy, then strain through the rag of Misconception. Cork up in the bottle of Malevolence, and hang on a skein of Street-Yarn. Shake occasionally for a few days, and it will be fit for use. Take a few drops before walking out and you will be prepared to speak all manner of evil, and that continually. This recipe has never been known to fail.

INDEX.

CAKES.

Name	Page
Boston, from 1 to 2	23
Bride, from 1 to 2	23
Buckeye, from 1 to 2	23
Chocolate, from 1 to 3	13
Clay, from 1 to 2	23
Cocoanut, from 1 to 12	12
Corn starch, from 1 to 8	9
Cottage, from 1 to 3	24
Cream and custard, from 1 to 8	11
Cup, from 1 to 8	15
Delicate, from 1 to 5	14
Dover, from 1 to 5	22
Feather, from 1 to 8	15
French, from 1 to 4	20
Fruit, from 1 to 19	6
Ice cream, from 1 to 2	23
Jelly, from 1 to 22	10
Lemon, from 1 to 5	18
Marble, from 1 to 8	5
Molasses cake or gingerbread, from 1 to 26	19
Mountain, from 1 to 14	16
Nut, from 1 to 4	15
Orange, from 1 to 3	18
Pearl, from 1 to 3	24
Pound, from 1 to 10	8
Railroad, from 1 to 2	24
Soda, from 1 to 3	23
Silver and gold, from 1 to 11	13
Snow, from 1 to 5	21
Spanish, from 1 to 3	22
Spice, from 1 to 5	21
Sponge, from 1 to 19	8
Surprise, from 1 to 3	24
Sweet William, from 1 to 2	21
Sugar, from 1 to 9	17
Straw, from 1 to 2	23
Tea, from 1 to 6	22
Tip-top, from 1 to 2	22
White and black, from 1 to 8	17

MISCELLANEOUS.

Name	Page
Almond	27
Anonymous	26
Apies	28
Aunt Jemima's	26
Bernard	26
Best cake in the world	26
Black dough	26
Bread	25
Breakfast	29
Center	26
Cheap	28
Cider	29
Citron	25
Clove	25
Coffee	28
Composition	28
Cousin's	28
Editor's	28
Elegant	26
Farmer's	28
Fourth	29
Good	27
Governor's	25
Guess	25
Harrison	25
Home	25
Honey	27
Huckleberry	27
Invalids'	29
Irish rag	25
Jenny Lind	27
Jenny Lind	29
Lady	28
Lady	25
Lafayette	26
Light	29
Lizzie's	25
Loaf	27
Log cabin	26
Matrimonial	27
Measure	28
Metropolitan	28
Miss Barton's	26
Neapolitan	27
Number	25
Poor man's	26
Pork	25
Puff	26
Queen	28
Rice	25
Rich seed	27
Rochester	29
Rough	26
Social	26
Taylor	29
Temperance	27
Union	28
Union	28
Walnut	27
Washington	28
Watermelon	24
Wedding	27
Yeast	28
Yellow	26

ICINGS.

Name	Page
From 1 to 6	29

CHOCOLATE CARAMELS.

Name	Page
From 1 to 3	29

SMALL CAKES.

Name	Page
Bunns, from 1 to 5	34
Cookies, from 1 to 16	30
Cream	35
Doughnuts, from 1 to 10	35
Drop, from 1 to 15	33
Ginger, from 1 to 21	32
Jumbles, from 1 to 12	31
Kisses	35
Potato	36
Sand, from 1 to 4	33
Scotch, from 1 to 2	33
Snow balls	33
Sugar pretzels	33
Taylor, from 1 to 5	31
Vanity	36

PUDDINGS.

Name	Page
Bread, from 1 to 5	36
Cottage, from 1 to 2	37
Queen of, from 1 to 4	36
Rice, from 1 to 4	37
Sauce for cottage	39
Suet, from 1 to 2	37
Tapioca, from 1 to 2	37

MISCELLANEOUS.

Name	Page
Apple citron	39
Apple tapioca	38
Batter	38
Bird's nest	38
Charlotte Russe	39
Corn starch	39
Cream tapioca	38
Egg	38
English	39
Fayette	38
Fig	39
Float	38
German puffs	38
Kiss or dandy	39
Lemon	38
Minute	38
Molasses	39
Orange	40
Potato	38
Pudding sauce	39
Snowden	39
Steam	39
Tyler	39
Welsh	40

CREAMS, CUSTARDS, ETC.

Name	Page
Lemon custards, from 1 to 4	40
Pumpkin custard, from 1 to 2	40
Velvet creams, from 1 to 2	40

MISCELLANEOUS CUSTARDS, CREAMS, ETC.

Name	Page
Apple cream	41
Apple custard	42
Apple snow	42
Buttermilk custard	41
Buttermilk custard	42
Charlotte Russe	41
Cocoanut custard	41
Gelatine	42
Float	41
Frozen custard	41
Orange dessert	42
Potato custard	41
Potato custard	42
Rogard	41
Snow balls	42
Strawberry ice cream	42
Vanilla cream	41

PIES.

Name	Page
Crumb pies, from 1 to 3	44
Crust for lemon custard	45
Golden pies, from 1 to 3	43
Lemon, from 1 to 6	42
Lemon custard, from 1 to 3	43
Mince pies, from 1 to 2	43
Mince pies, without meat	44
Mock mince pies	44
Patent mince pies	44
Sugar pies, from 1 to 3	44

MISCELLANEOUS.

Name	Page
Berry or fruit shortcake	45
Cream pie	44
Cream custard pie	45
Delicate pie	45
Ginger pie	44
Molasses pie	45
Oyster pie	44
Pumpkin pie	45
Quince tarts	45
Shoo Fly pie	45
Shoo Fly pie	45
Spice pie	45
Strawberry shortcake	45
Sweet potato pie	44
Vinegar pie	

EGGS.
Apple omelet 46
Omelet with dried beef. 46
Omelets, from 1 to 5............... 46
Snow balls............................... 46
Ruffled eggs 46

BREAD.
Rusks, from 1 to 5.................. 46

BISCUIT.
American biscuit..................... 47
Apple fritters.......................... 49
Cheap flannel cakes................ 49
Corn batter cakes.................... 48
Corn bread, from 1 to 7.......... 48
Cream biscuit 47
Corn cakes to eat when warm, 48
Corn pone, from 1 to 3........... 49
Good waffles........................... 49
Hard times biscuit 47
Potato biscuit 47
Pounded biscuit 47
Snap buckwheat cakes............ 49
Soda biscuit, from 1 to 3......... 47
Sugar biscuit........................... 47
Sweet waffles.......................... 49
Tea biscuit............................... 47
Waffles, from 1 to 3................. 48

MUFFINS.
Corn muffins, from 1 to 2 50
French rolls or twist................ 49
Graham bread.......................... 50
Madison rolls........................... 50
Mush cakes.............................. 50
Potato muffins......................... 50
Potato rolls.............................. 50
Puff muffins............................. 49
Sally Lunn............................... 49
Vanities................................... 49
Water crackers........................ 50
Wiggs....................................... 50

MEATS.
Beef steak................................ 50
Ham toast................................ 50
Minced beef............................. 51
Mince-meats............................ 51
Sausage, to preserve................ 50
Veal cutlets.............................. 50

FISH.
Cod-fish balls.......................... 51
Eels, fried................................ 51
Fried fish 51
Oysters, scolloped 51

SOUPS.
Beef 51
Potato 52
Tomato.................................... 51
Vegetable 52

SAUCES.
Chili 52
Foam.. 52
Lemon...................................... 52

KETCHUPS.
Cucumber, from 1 to 3............ 52
Tomato, from 1 to 4................ 52

PICKLES.
Cantaloupe pickles, from 1 to 2, 55
Cherries................................... 56
Cucumber pickles, from 1 to 3, 54
Blackberries 56
Flint pickles............................ 55
Green tomato p., from 1 to 6... 55
Lily, from 1 to 2...................... 53
Peaches, from 1 to 4................ 53
Spanish 54
Tomato chowder..................... 56
Tomato higdon........................ 56
To preserve p. from specks.... 57
Walnut pickles........................ 56
Yellow pickles......................... 57

CORN, VEGETABLES, ETC.
Beans, baked........................... 58
Cabbage, stuffed..................... 58
Cauliflower.............................. 58
Corn, canned, from 1 to 2....... 57
Corn oysters, from 1 to 6........ 57
Potato cakes............................ 58
Potatoes cooked...................... 58
Potatoes, Saratoga.................. 58
Potatoes, sweet, made of Irish
  potatoes 58
Tomatoes, fried....................... 58
Tomatoes, scolloped 59
Tomatoes, smothered.............. 58

SALADS, ETC.
Chicken salads, from 1 to 2.... 59
Cold slaw................................. 59
Cold slaw, dressing for........... 59
Turnip slaw............................. 59

CANNED FRUIT.
Grapes..................................... 59
Peaches................................... 59
Strawberries 60

PRESERVES, FRUITS, JELLIES, ETC.
Apple jelly............................... 60
Apple jelly, dried.................... 60
Blackberry preserves.............. 60
Damsons, to preserve............. 60
Gooseberry jelly...................... 60
Peaches for pies, preserved.... 60
Pine apple jam........................ 60
Quince marmalade.................. 60
Strawberry jelly...................... 60

DRINKS.
Beer 62
Beer, cream tartar................... 62
Beer, for making..................... 61
Beer, ginger............................. 62
Beer, sugar.............................. 61
Beer, to make.......................... 62
Cordial, raspberry................... 61
Pop, ginger, from 1 to 2.......... 61
Shrub, blackberry................... 62
Syrup, blackberry................... 62
Syrup, lemon........................... 62
Sherbet, patent gas................. 61
Wine, blackberry, from 1 to 2, 62
Wine, currant.......................... 61
Wine, elderberry..................... 62
Vinegar, cherry....................... 61
Vinegar, raspberry.................. 61

MISCELLANEOUS.
Ants, to destroy...................... 63
Ants, to drive away red.......... 63
Bed-bugs, how to exterminate, 63
Bluing, liquid.......................... 64
Blacking, liquid 64
Breakfast dish......................... 65
Butter, to preserve 2 years..... 64
Cancer wart, to remove........... 64
Carpet, to patch old................ 64
Cement, superior.................... 64
Cocoanut candy, quickly made, 65
Cologne, fine cheap................. 64
Cough syrup............................ 64
Cream drops, chocolate.......... 65
Gloves, to clean white leather, 65
Grease, to remove................... 63
Fit of passion, cure for a........ 65
Ink, indelible.......................... 64
Ink stains, to remove.............. 63
Lace, to renew old black......... 64
Mildew, to remove.................. 63
Moths in carpets, to prevent.. 64
Peach leather.......................... 65
Polish for glass, silver, &c..... 64
Powder, baking....................... 64
Rising to keep long, for 65
Rust, how to take out 65
Soap... 63
Soap, erasive........................... 63
Soap, hard............................... 63
Soap, how to make.................. 62
Snake bite, cure for................ 66
Spitting blood......................... 65
Stains out of mahogany, to take 63
Stains, to remove.................... 63
Stove, to clean the inside of a. 65
Tattlers, a recipe for making.. 65
Toast, French 65
Toast, German........................ 65
Vinegar................................... 64
Wrinkles, cure for................... 65
Yeast, an excellent.................. 64

About the Author

Tom Kelchner is a retired journalist, technical writer and blogger who has lived within 20 miles of Newville, Pa., for much of his life. He has had a passionate interest in the everyday cooking and baking of many ethnic traditions – especially those found in Pennsylvania.

He has hiked the ridgelines that define Cumberland County, cycled the country roads and trails and enjoyed the produce, meats, cheeses, beer and wine of the region. Over the years he spent countless joyful hours with friends on farms near Newville picnicking, cooking outdoors and picking huckleberries, mushrooms and grapes.

As the author of *To Great Grandmother's House We Go*, he became familiar with Pennsylvania Dutch and historic American recipes. He also became familiar with the vast food history research possibilities in community and charity cookbooks such as the *Cumberland Valley Cook and General Recipe Book*.

He was inspired to trace the origins of older recipes by the works of Pennsylvania food scholars William Wos Weaver and Becky Libourel Diamond.

Mr. Kelchner lives and cooks with his wife Linda (who bakes a lot) in Carlisle, Pa., eleven miles from Newville. He writes about food at PaFoodLife.com.

www.ingramcontent.com/pod-product-compliance
Lightning Source LLC
Chambersburg PA
CBHW072221070526
44585CB00015B/1442